SCARRED
4 PURPOSE
ON PURPOSE

Shonda Boyd Brown

Copyright © 2022 Shonda Boyd Brown

ALL RIGHTS RESERVED. This book contains material protected under International and Federal Copyright Laws and Treaties. Any unauthorized reprint or use of this material is prohibited. No part of this book may be reproduced or transmitted in any form or by any means, electronic or mechanical, including photocopying, recording, or by any information storage and retrieval system without express written permission from the author/publisher.

Unless otherwise noted, all Scripture quotations are taken from The Bible Gateway Online. All rights reserved.

Book Cover Design: Prize Publishing House

Printed by: Prize Publishing House, LLC in the United States of America.

First printing edition 2022.

Prize Publishing House
P.O. Box 9856 Chesapeake, VA 23321
www.PrizePublishingHouse.com

Library of Congress Control Number: 2021912551

ISBN (Paperback): 978-1-7371829-7-9
ISBN (E-Book): 978-1-7371829-8-6

Contents

Endorsements v
Acknowledgements ix
Dedication xiii
Foreword xv
Introduction xvii

Chapter 1   God Sets The Scene 1
Chapter 2   The Suffering Will Build Character 23
Chapter 3   Don't Abort The Process 42
Chapter 4   Remodeled For Purpose 55
Chapter 5   It's Time for a Reset 65
Chapter 6   Elevation Is Undeniable 73
Chapter 7   The Divine Assignment 77
Chapter 8   The Unstoppable You 85

Conclusion 89
Salvation Prayer 91
About the Author 93

Endorsements

An oyster, when it's irritated, releases an internal substance that creates a pearl. Most oysters endure the irritation again to make yet another pearl. No wonder pearls are Shonda's favorite accessory! Her life and the processes that she has endured are synonymous with that of the oyster. If you have endured what seems to be trial after trial and disappointment after disappointment, you would appreciate the wisdom that Prophetess Shonda Brown shares to help you understand the role that pain plays in your life and still be able to live life on purpose! We celebrate that you are no longer wounded from your past; you are scab-free and scarred for purpose on purpose.

Pastor Anthony and Lady Byrdzetta Knotts
Embassy Church, Greensboro, NC

Endorsements

The time has come for you to manifest and learn how you can allow God to use your past pain and traumas for purpose, on purpose! Prophetess Shonda Boyd Brown has used her personal life experiences and encounters with pain to walk in power, wisdom, freedom, and creativity. Prophetess Brown shows us how God can take what the enemy meant for evil and turn it around for our good. In this book, *Scarred 4 Purpose on Purpose*, you will learn that every situation you have gone through was preparation for your purpose, as she teaches you how to use pain as fuel for you to now help someone else. All you must do is trust God and go through the process and not faint. We highly recommend this book because of the transparency and heartfelt message of becoming all God has created in you. Your life will be shifted by this truly God-fearing, anointed woman of God.

Pastor Isaac L. Settle
Evangelist Shyra L. Settle

Acknowledgements

For all those that held me accountable by constantly reminding me to complete my book, it is finally here. Thank you for the push and all of your prayers and support!

Thank you, Abba Father, for being the sustainer of my mind and the keeper of my soul. I'm indebted to you. #GODSGIRL

To my why, my heart, my mini-me, my favorite actress, and my favorite model, the one GOD saw fit to bless me with during a time I needed you the most: Zakiya Lashone' Brown. You were and still are my reason I need to keep me going, my real-life Barbie doll. Thanks for being the love I needed on many cloudy days. You brought the sunshine and gave me the strength to live through it because I knew your little eyes were watching everything I did. My job was to try to be a good example to you. I hope you know how proud I am of you and all of your accomplishments. When praying about my foreword, you were instantly placed in my spirit; you are such a wise young lady. I thank God for you. It's us against the world for life! Mommy loves you so much, and you will FOREVER BE MY BABY.

Mom, thank you for being my nurturer and confidante and for standing strong with me in my process. I can only imagine your thoughts as a mother seeing your only child go through such a tumultuous season. With your prayers and encouragement, I made it out. I love you dearly, and I pray GOD'S best blessings upon your life. Thanks for all you have done!

Daddy, thanks for validating me as a little girl and for your prayers, love, and support. Thanks for all you have done! I love you dearly.

My goddaughters, Chelsea and Chasitei, I'm so grateful for you both, a position I've never taken lightly. You both have respected me and loved me as your godmother. I pray that I have and will continue to be a godly example in your life. Thanks for being my why and my heart. I love you both immeasurably.

To my B.F.F/Sister/Ride or Die Pamela, aka my Shugga Bean, our steps were truly ordered the day we met in the break room at Harris Teeter our senior year of high school. You are the world's best godmother, a friend that sticks closer than a sister, and truly the sister I never had. Thanks for consistently being there for my daughter and me, for being a blessing to us in so many ways, and for always loving and being so supportive in everything we do. Thanks for being that listening ear and my accountability partner. Thanks for allowing me to be the godmother to my beautiful goddaughters. Last but not least, thanks for sharing your mother, who loved me as her own. "Josie" is truly missed, and I truly wish she was here to celebrate this moment. She let me know I was anointed for real (LOL). She trusted me to pray for her, "Shon Shon, do your thang." I love you dearly, my Shug!

To my late Godfather, Robert Pulliam, I miss you. I truly hate that you are not here to celebrate this moment with me. Ma Pulliam, I thank you both for planting a seed in my life, making me live up to a standard that would ultimately lead me to be the God-fearing woman

I am today. Thanks for treating me as your own and opening your home to me. I love you dearly!

To my B.F.F./ God sister Sonja, when you saw one, you saw the other; I promise you couldn't tell us anything growing up. I'm so thankful for the genuine and consistent authentic years of friendship, sisterhood, love, support, and for being that listening ear. Thanks for unselfishly sharing your parents, home, room, and food with me (LOL); you being a picky eater meant more food for me. I love you dearly. You are forever my sister; blood couldn't make us any closer.

To Phyllis Carter, thanks for being a part of my sisterhood since middle school. The years of memories, support, laughter, and tears will always be cherished.

To Wanda Moravian-Hobson (aka's Shugga Mama), thanks, Sis, for being a part of my village and allowing me to be a part of yours as well. Your love and support have truly been appreciated. I love you dearly.

To all of my grandparents, I miss you all so much and wish you all were here to celebrate this momentous occasion with me. You all played such a significant part in my growth and the woman I am today. I had the best grandparents ever and was so blessed to spend time with you all. I love you all dearly!

> Ira & Ethel Shoffner
> John & Dorothy Boyd
> Allen & Ethel Brown
> Beulah Hickman

To all my family! Aunts, uncles, and cousins, I love you dearly!

Aunt Helen, thank you for all of your love, support, encouragement, and prayers! It has meant so much to me.

My spiritual daughters and mentees, you rock! I'm so grateful for each and every one of you. You all know who you are. Much love!

To all of my clients (church members) lol, thank you for your love, support, and patience. Love you all!

Bishop Anthony & Lady Byrdzetta Knotts, thanks for providing me a cave when I needed it the most. Thanks for the push and for not allowing me to stay stuck. Your love, friendship, and leadership will never be forgotten. Love you dearly!

To the best Elect Ladies & Pastor Sisters on this side, you all mean so much to me. Thanks for your love, prayers, encouragement, and support.

> Lady Erica Poteat
> Lady Laverne Alexander
> Apostle Antoinette Waddell
> Prophetess Lynn Watkins

Dedication

I dedicate this book to four lovely ladies I was privileged to service for years. You all were so faithful in supporting my business. While in the salon, you witnessed my transformation and embraced who I had become in Christ. I was able to impact your lives and witness you suffer through your own personal wounds, and you did it gracefully. You will never be forgotten. You are truly missed. You were Scarred 4 Purpose On Purpose!

Love You Always.

>Linda Sweezer
>Sherry Massey
>Renee' Whitsett
>Juuanna Morehead

Foreword

To say I am proud of the author of this masterpiece would simply be an understatement. Likewise, to say that I am surprised at the outcome of this masterpiece would simply be dishonest. For years, I've watched her prolong releasing her story and always wondered why. Now I finally realize it was for a divine purpose. The timing was just right; we still needed to witness the comeback story. As cliche as it may sound, there is always a happy ending, but for the author of this book, I would like to refer to it as a happy beginning and this time the right way, this time with experience, this time healed, this time free of all bondage, this time she's READY!

One of the strongest individuals I know, I have been able to watch her firsthand overcome each and every obstacle thrown her way and watched her overcome them all with class and grace. As she lives by the motto, "Never look like what you're going through."

Who would've known somebody who is still filled with so much love and so much compassion has weathered so many storms? The beauty of it all is that though it hurt her, though it threw her off at times, she didn't stay there, and I am forever grateful for that.

She chose to get up and fight back for me and not only for me but for you too. To show us that we could also go through the fire and not smell like smoke, not turn to coal but to come out a diamond.

Mommy, thank you! Thank you for getting up. I needed you. The world needed you. Looking back, I hope you never doubt that what you went through was strategic and was simply you being ordained to guide women to their path of freedom.

Words will never be able to describe how proud I am of you for releasing your baby to the world. I pray for nothing but success and blessings as you embark upon this new journey of being a #1 selling author.

Ladies, you are in for a treat. Prepare to be delivered, prepare to be awakened, prepare to be FREE because you were Scarred for Purpose.

- Zakiya L. Brown

Introduction

OH WOW! I finally get to see this prophecy come to pass. Yet though the vision tarries, you must learn how to wait on God's timing. The time has finally come. I have been called to the kingdom for such a time as this! I believe what we have experienced as a nation has given validity to this book. We have experienced the worst pandemic the world has seen arguably in 100 years. COVID-19 has claimed many lives, and this virus has left many wounded in every aspect of life.

On March 16, 2020, North Carolina and most states shut down, and guess what? It was my 49th birthday. What you and I knew as normal changed suddenly right before our eyes. We were on lockdown. Schools were going virtual; businesses were closing, some permanently. People were figuring out how to set up space in their homes to work remotely, while others were unemployed. We could not find household essentials like toilet tissue, Clorox, and Lysol spray and wipes. Death tolls were rising faster than the medical experts could keep up with. This season was full of social isolation, higher mental health illnesses, depression, and anxiety. Suicidal thoughts skyrocketed, marriages suffered, and domestic abuse increased. Before the pandemic, we never really heard phrases like "quarantining and social distancing" and staying six feet apart to control the spread of the virus. We typically saw people wearing masks in hospital facilities, but now they are an important and necessary addition to our wardrobe.

This global pandemic has left many trying to heal from something we did not see coming, a moment in time we will never forget. This reminds me of my personal story that changed the trajectory of my life that left me wounded, seemingly beyond repair, or so I thought. The pandemic has left many perplexed about how to feel and how to heal. Where do we go from here? We have been completely caught off guard, not prepared for the pandemic, social injustice, police brutality, or systemic racism that has heightened all in the same year. What a year to remember! I find peace and solitude knowing that even though we were surprised, it did not surprise our God because He is all-knowing (omniscient), He is everywhere (omnipresent), and He is all-powerful (omnipotent).

God knows everything and has the power to do anything but fail us. So do not allow what you hear, feel, or see to decrease your faith and leave you in a place of hopelessness. God knows how to take the bad and turn it for our good. *"And we know that all things work together for good to them that love God, to them who are the called according to his purpose"* (Romans 8:28, KJV). I have learned that there are reasons and seasons that God allows some of the most devastating events to occur in our lives. Unfortunately, we do not get to choose the season that is suitable or comfortable for our flesh. *"To everything, there is a season and a time to every purpose under Heaven"* (Ecclesiastes 3:1, KJV). Selah! Now, pause and think about that.

God does all things for a purpose, on purpose. You will never find purpose absent from a wound. The beautiful part about a wound is that it heals with proper care and time; all wounds turn into scars telling stories and holding memories. Every scar is fashionably knitted together for a purpose. God created us with purpose in mind, and you will do yourself a disservice to leave this earth without knowing why He created you and who He created you for.

In this book, *Scarred 4 Purpose on Purpose*, I share my journey. I wrote this book praying that you would be inspired, motivated, empowered, and equipped to push through your pain, find your purpose, and live a life that forgives. Prayerfully, you will find your confidence and understand that your value and worth are far greater than rubies. When you discover this, you will have the courage to walk away from abuse, unhealthy relationships, and anything that will hinder you from being who God has created you to be, even if it means letting go of your own self-sabotage; self-inflicted wounds are the worse, they will keep you in wounded places longer than you should be. Never get too comfortable with a place God has called you to pass through, and you make the decision to park all because it feels good, and you don't want to deal with the shame of walking away or putting in the work that it will take to heal. Don't deny yourself the freedom you know you deserve. If you find yourself constantly trying to prove your worth to someone, you have already forgotten your value. Knowing my self-worth and value is what caused me to walk away from my marriage of 22 years.

Before I continue, please let me say this, this is my story, not yours. I am not saying for you to leave your marriage. I love marriage, and I respect marriage, but what I am saying is know your worth, don't settle, and do what's best for you and your safety. If you need an answer on what to do, seek God first as I did for His wisdom. As you read this book, there are some things I want you to know that I believe will help you on this journey called life. There are words in your wounds; those words are wisdom. We have all heard the saying, "Learn from others' experiences." I constantly share with my daughter, "If mommy has gone through it and graduated with honors from it, why must you try it." There are times you must submit to someone else's wisdom, especially if you have seen them go through it and there's proof. You need to listen and learn.

One of my favorite stories in the Bible is about Ruth and Naomi. Here you find Naomi wounded because she had lost everything dear to her heart, husband, and sons. As a result of her pain, she chooses to be called "Mara," which means "bitter." She wanted to be identified by her pain, telling her daughters-in-law she had nothing to offer them. In reality, she did; she was just too wounded to see it. Often times when we are wounded by losses, it looks like there is nothing left, and the truth is we have more to offer after we experience the loss than before the loss. She had lived such an impactful life in front of them as a God-fearing mother, wife, and mother-in-law that not even her being bitter would turn them away. They were determined to follow her, and they replied, "We will go with you." Naomi dissuades them three times. The third time, Orpah leaves, but Ruth stays. Ruth chooses to submit to wisdom. Naomi's relationship with God made an impact on Ruth. *"And Ruth said, 'Intreat me not to leave thee, or to return from following after thee: for whither thou goest, I will go; and where thou lodgest, I will lodge: thy people shall be my people, and thy God my God: Where thou diest, will I die, and there will I be buried: the LORD do so to me, and more also, if ought but death part thee and me'"* (Ruth 1:16-17, KJV). Naomi's wound led her to her Kinsman Redeemer, known as Boaz.

The pain that you endured will lead someone else to their promise. You must be connected to a voice during the dark seasons of your life, and I am not just talking about any voice. I am talking about a voice that speaks wisdom with an ear to hear God.

Another thing we see in this story, God has people assigned to you that are watching how you handle the storms of life. Yes, through scripture, we see Naomi was in her feelings. We have all been there before when we do not understand the reasoning behind our suffering. I believe she finally realized she was not going through this pain for herself. God used this derailment to push her to a greater purpose. If God allows us to go through it, He will bring us out greater than before. I did question why I was going through it. I felt as though I did not deserve the sentence that was given to me. But I learned later that it was never about me, and neither is it about you. Ruth watched how Naomi handled her dark season. As it was with me, I had my daughter and others watching me, and so shall it be with you. Others are watching how you will handle the dark seasons. If you hold on long enough, it will all make sense.

As you read the story of Naomi and Ruth, they were sustained by gleaning kernels from the barley harvest. Ruth married Boaz all because she chose to follow wisdom. You must learn how to be content in dark seasons. *"…I have learned, in whatever state I am, to be content"* (Philippians 4:11, KJV).

Dark seasons will show your level of contentment. Orpah showed discontentment. She also rejected the chance to follow God when she separated from Naomi and Ruth. She went back to what was familiar to her. She went back to Moab; her returning to Moab led to a life of more darkness and despair. It's imperative that you don't let the pain of the wound separate you from God in dark seasons. Remain connected to those with the wisdom you need to survive, glean, and be content in that place. I believe that your level of contentment will reflect your level of gratitude. We have to be grateful for everything, the good and the bad. It's impossible to develop contentment without gratitude. You will know you have them both because you will begin to focus on what's left and not what was a loss.

The reality was Naomi was old. She was childless, could not have any more kids, and was bitter. But what she had left was a relationship with God. It's not until you lose everything that you notice what you have left is more valuable than what you thought you needed. Ruth was content. She showed gratitude for what was left. She stayed committed and connected to Naomi and her God until she understood her assignment, walked in her assignment, fulfilled her purpose, and lived in her promise. She became the great-grandmother of King David. God honored her integrity and loyalty. Ruth followed her heart and her influence increased by doing what was right in a painful season. So, whatever you may be going through, endure the process. You are here for a specific reason. (Consider it nothing but joy, my brothers, and sisters, whenever you fall into various trials. Be assured that the testing of your faith (through experience) produces endurance (leading to spiritual maturity) and inner peace) (James 1:2, AMP).

CHAPTER 1

God Sets The Scene

~

*"For I know the plans I have for you, declares the
Lord, 'plans to prosper you and not to harm you,
plans to give you hope and a future."'*

(Jeremiah 29:11, NIV)

For I know the plans I have for you, says God! And nothing can stop my plan. When God sets the scene, He has a goal in mind. He is the producer and executive producer of your lifetime story. God has strategically set your stage specifically for you for His glory. He is aware of the plot and the plot twist because He wrote it. He has used you to display His miraculous power. Have you ever felt like you're sitting on top of the world, excited about life, and suddenly, it seems like your story is changing right before your eyes? You notice it isn't going the way you had planned it out in your mind, and the overwhelming feeling of being disappointed and frustrated starts to take over your emotions. You notice that the producer has changed the scene, adversity comes, financial hardship comes, you lose that loved one, you lose that job, you lose that friendship, your marriage starts to fail, which leads to separation or divorce, your children begin to challenge you with their behavior, your body is attacked with sickness or disease, and your business starts to suffer. Don't be alarmed; the plot twist was added to get you better acquainted with the Creator, the One who specializes in wounded and broken people. Sometimes the only way He can get our attention is through pain and trouble. Being broken is definitely designed to teach you humility. The closer we get to Him, the better we understand who we are, whose we are, and our purpose. It may look like you are on the road to failure, and there is no hope; God has handpicked you to grow through what you may be experiencing. God loves using broken people, and perhaps you have been called to the kingdom for such a time as this. You have been hidden, and you will be the next best secret that God is getting ready to showcase after this.

In the book of Esther, you will find a story that God penned way before she was born, a story displaying the bravery of a young girl who had childhood trauma that would one day lead her to become "The Queen." She was an orphan who once lived in exile, was taken captive, her virginity was taken, and she was willing to take a risk by putting her life on the line for her people. Esther comes into her adoptive cousins, and some say Uncle Mordecai's life, wounded from childhood trauma, never knowing her parents. It was said that her father died before she was born, and her mother died giving birth. Esther finds herself immediately being groomed as a teenager to take the position of the former "Queen Vashti," who refused to show up to the king's party as entertainment for him and his drunk friends. Her refusal was a setup for the next queen.

Mordecai, a man of faith who adopts the future queen, becomes her biggest cheerleader, seeing in her what she doesn't see in herself.

He assures her by creating a safe place in their relationship that he can be trusted. He sees a problem that he believed only Esther could solve. However, I can only imagine her daily battles of questioning if she could do what seemed impossible and if he could really be trusted, along with her feeling the pain and the emptiness from being an orphan.

An "orphan spirit" will leave an empty void in your life. It invades the mind, bringing so many mixed emotions, such as abandonment, loneliness, and isolation, often leaving you with feelings of insecurity, competitiveness, seeking attention, wanting to stand out, and being overly compensated for material possessions. It is very difficult to maintain healthy relationships and to receive love. Those who grew up without their parents or have been abandoned or rejected by their parents often treat those that try to love them as if they were the ones who hurt them. This person seeks to find their own identity and often wonders where they fit in; they usually don't adhere to leadership or take advice well from others. Esther defies the norm for a greater good. She embraced what was, and she experienced God's love and sovereignty.

Esther's story is a reminder that God will heal, restore, remove, and replace; even when you don't feel or see Him in the battle with you, be encouraged that He's always there. He chose a young woman who seemingly lost it all, her parents, freedom, and virginity. But what she gained was so much more from the pain she endured. Her inadequacies or yours will not change His mind concerning the plan He has for your life just because you have them. In fact, it's the opposite; your inability to perform is what sets the stage and draws Him to you.

This is your time to embrace and own everything that has happened in your childhood. It happened, so get over it and let it go; yes, I said it; it's hindering you. If you don't like the adult you have become, look back at your childhood. Whether good or bad, your childhood experiences will be the foundation upon which your adult lives are built. It is a part of you, and it plays an important role in your story. God wants to use all the drama, trauma, and those blocked-out memories you try to avoid remembering because they are too painful. Many of you have allowed your past to control your future, and it's suffocating the life out of you; a slow death is taking place. Remove the mask and accept what it is so that you may experience God's redemptive power. It's time to be made whole. Don't allow the enemy to continue to steal from you. *"The thief cometh not, but for to steal, and to kill and to destroy; I am come that they might have life, and that they might have it more abundantly"* (John 10:10, KJV).

Nothing catches God by surprise. *"For as the heavens are higher than the earth, so are my ways higher than your ways, and my thoughts higher than your thoughts"* (Isaiah 55:9, NKJV). For all the analytical thinking people that have to see it before you see it, this mindset will hinder your growth and faith in God. The worst thing you can do is try to figure God out when He has already written the narrative of our lives. Just as Esther's situation looked impossible, my situation looked impossible. And it will always look impossible when your life is out of your control. You will have to learn how to work on what you can control. I couldn't control who He wanted to use or what He wanted to use. You will never know the who, what, when, or the how, but you will discover the "why" from what He allows to break you. Your "why" is what matters in the end. Stay in your process long enough for Him to show you your "why." Your "why" is the reason you survived, you exist, and you will survive. Esther's why was discovered. God used Mordecai to save her; He used her to save the Jews. We must trust Him with our broken pieces.

Several years ago, I was in a movie and received an IMDb credit as an actress. I was asked to take a role as a pastor in the movie "The Present," which had amazing producers and an interesting plot and plot twist. My role did come with a script, but I was told to flow as if it were a Sunday morning service. I share this because God wants to get us from acting out a script to being the script. It's easy to act it out, but the hard part is becoming one with the script and being mature enough to study and live by His scripted word. I found out quickly that I had no say in my kingdom role because He knew the plan and expected end He had for me, according to Jeremiah 29:11. I found this chapter of Jeremiah interesting. We must understand this scripture that we love to quote because it seems to give us hope in painful and dark seasons. It's encouraging to know that God has a plan for us that is good, and the suffering that we will and are experiencing won't last long.

We ignore the scriptures above the eleventh verse. (A quick study tip suggestion: if you don't understand a verse you are reading in your Bible, start reading at the beginning of your chapter to gain more clarity.) If we read the verses before that one that we love to quote, we will see that the Israelites were taken into exile and given over to the Babylonians for seventy years; they were given a promise that wasn't going to be fulfilled until after the exile. In verses five and six, God gives them instructions on how to survive while they're in exile: "Your exile will be long; build houses and live in them, (plan to stay) plant gardens and eat the food they produce." He tells them to grow in number, marry their kids off, multiply there, increase, and become greater in the dark seasons. He then releases the assignment. In verse seven, He tells them to pray and seek peace and prosperity in the place that He deported them to. As they prospered because you prayed, you will prosper while you are in exile. This is interesting that God tells them to pray and desire peace for the same persons He allowed to take them into captivity. Pray for those who have and will despitefully use you, harm you, and talk about you while you're in your place of exile. Be careful not to pray for their destruction because you can easily be affected by it. God desires that you live peaceably with others and be content in the place He has you.

In verses eight and nine, He tells them not to pay attention to the false prophets and fortune-tellers in the land of Babylon to trick them. "Do not listen to their dreams because they are telling you lies in my name. I have not sent them, says the Lord." Beware of those that will tell you something that God didn't say. When you are in dark seasons, you are very vulnerable and can draw unwanted spirits out of your desperation. If God says stay, don't move before your time. STAY in EXILE! He is God, and He will tell you when to move; He will bring you to your promise at its appointed time. In verse ten, the promise is released. Thus says the Lord, "When seventy years are completed for Babylon, I will come to you and fulfill my good promise to bring you back to this place." Now, verse eleven says: "I know the plans I have for you says the Lord." So, we see they were in exile for seventy long years before the promise. What happens when the place you're in and your plans don't look like His plans? What do you do when things don't end the way you planned, or when you find yourself in a less than ideal space for longer than you wanted? Proverbs 16:9, NKJV spells it out beautifully: *"In their hearts, man plans their course but the Lord establishes their steps."* You will have to blossom and flourish where you are. Everyone that has ever experienced an elevation in the kingdom of God was first exiled from somewhere.

GOD SETS MY SCENE

~

In 1991, on a nice hot summer day in the barbershop, while waiting for my little cousin to get a haircut, a gentleman sitting in the barber chair caught my attention quickly. He reminded me of an Idris Elba or Morris Chestnut, at least so I thought, the man was "fine." As the barber turned his chair, he made contact with my hands and began to compliment them. As he made small talk with me, I checked him out thoroughly. He was tall, slender built, with dark chocolate pretty skin, pearly white teeth, and dressed as I liked, not to mention this man's cologne smelled so good that it almost put me into a trance. He began to ask me did I want my car detailed, and of course, you know the answer was yes. He proceeded to hand me his business card and asked when I wanted it done. I answered as soon as he was available. He wasn't just good-looking; I would eventually learn he was intelligent and talented, and he loved God, he immediately expressed his love for God, and he had a lot of potential. (Disclaimer: I do not think it's wise to marry anyone based on potential alone; see that potential in action before you get into a commitment.) As for myself, yeah, I had it going on, slim and trim, intelligent, fresh out of beauty school, working in a salon, later becoming a platform artist and hair educator, pursuing my passion, and let's just say money wasn't a problem at all.

I was building my clientele, enjoying the newfound freedom as an entrepreneur, building my empire as a single woman, credit was looking good, and confident in who I was and embracing who I was becoming. Above all, I was teachable. My mentor was Ms. Geraldine Moore. At the very first salon I worked in after beauty school, I was the youngest person in the salon at that time. In one of our empowering mentoring sessions, she said to me, "If you want to succeed in business, pay your tithe and give God his ten percent." I listened and found that out to be true. That alone cut years off of my learning curve because I obeyed and applied what I learned. I thought it was strange she didn't speak to me about being saved, knowing that she was indeed a lover of Christ. It was a setup; I followed her advice professionally and spiritually. I clubbed on Saturday night and was in church on Sunday morning at St. James Baptist church, paying my tithes and offering. I eventually became an active member, and later I would eventually get married at the same church. Applying biblical principles works. Not only did it keep my pockets full, but it would also later set me up for a relationship that I would eventually obtain with Christ through my faithful giving and my mentor being relentless about her witnessing to us about Christ and hell. I found out that you will eventually serve who and what you keep giving your money and time to. Pause for a moment and think about who and what you are giving your money and time to and how it has affected your life and others around you. You are a product of your seed. Sow with caution!

Moving right along to how God set this scene up for me, I was wounded to win. The platonic friendship that I had with my newfound crush at the age of nineteen turned into a date that turned into seven years of dating off and on. In those seven years, I began to collect data.

As a single woman, when you are dating, that is your time to collect data. How was he raised? Watch and see how he treats the women in his life. How is his credit? What is his religion? Does he desire to get married? Does he cook? Does he want kids? Create your list, don't settle, and ask a lot of questions when dating. It is vital. I learned things about him that I hated, I loved, and things I was willing to put up with because I wanted him. I was mentally, emotionally, and physically wired and eventually caught up in a sexual soul tie. Lust is real!

I was fully persuaded this could be my man for life. Our chemistry was great together. When he came around, my soul lit up. Have you ever felt this way about someone? However, in our dating, it wasn't long before I discovered his childhood trauma. His mother had passed at a young age, his dad wasn't really in his life, and he was raised by his God-fearing grandmother, which would later give me a greater understanding of how things played out in our marriage. I also discovered he wasn't ready to settle down, and what I thought was mine turned out to be the desire of every other female. That eventually led me to be a bit devilish at times because I felt as though he was rejecting me, and rejection never feels good when you want what you want. I didn't realize at the time that rejection is God's protection. As classy as I was, I was that girl that had that "don't play with me" attitude and a ride or die friend that was down to do whatever. We all need a bestie like that, and I'm forever grateful for mine (we didn't play games). However, this man knew how to hit the wrong buttons, which resulted in me letting my anger dictate my behavior. I cut up a few tires and threw bricks at his apartment door. One night, I even decided I would paint his brand-new GT Ford White Mustang with red lipstick, all because I wasn't getting the attention I wanted when I wanted it. It didn't take me long to snap back to myself after my fleshly reactions. I had that self-talk, "Girl, you are the treasure, and it's his job to chase after you. If indeed you are the one, he will come to find you, as he did in the first place."

I've never been an easy woman or a needy one. I didn't need a man; I wanted one, and there is a big, big difference. I was picky when it came to my men, but this relationship had my nose wide open, as the old folks would say. With that said, ladies, stop settling and being too easy, too available, and accessible to men when they are not trying to commit to you. Truth be told, men like a challenge, and they don't like anything too easy. I gave him the challenge he needed, and I pulled back. Know when to pull back and not be desperate. You can't make a man want you; I don't care what you do. Stop trying to be wives to boyfriends that just see you as a girlfriend or just a friend and, in some cases, just somewhere to lay his head. Men don't mind reaping the benefits of a wife and leaving your status the same. Sometimes we try to force things that we are not mentally or spiritually mature enough to handle.

You know how we do, ladies; we will start looking at our age, and the years we have been together and automatically think that's the time to plan a wedding. This is far from the truth -- trust God's timing. If you're not ready to be a wife and you haven't built your empire, stop asking God for a husband and get yourself together and allow

Him to prepare you. Marriage is work, and it's sacred, so you must be called to it and anointed for it. It's a covenant you are graced for, and everyone is not purposed for it. According to Matthew 19:11-12, MSG, "But Jesus said, 'not everyone is mature enough to live a married life, it requires a certain aptitude and grace.'" Marriage isn't for everyone. Some, from birth, seemingly never give marriage a thought. Others never get asked or accepted. And some decide not to get married for kingdom reasons. But if you're capable of growing into the largeness of marriage, do it. Marriage was designed to be a life of enlargement through multiplication, not just birthing babies but also birthing vision. Also understanding that marriage is the representation of the relationship with Christ and His people.

With that said, you need to pray and ask if it's His will for you to be married. After three and a half years of celibacy and isolation, God spoke to me while I was away on a business trip in New Jersey one night in the hotel room, and He told me I would be married and to who. On November 28, 1998, I was married and was led into captivity. I was excited and clueless all at the same time, not knowing what was ahead of me.

But it wasn't long before I found out why my three years of training as a single, saved, and satisfied woman were so intense. I had to be prepared for what was ahead. I couldn't have survived without my total commitment to Christ before marriage. 1 Corinthians 7:34 says that an unmarried woman or virgin is concerned about the Lord's affairs; Her aim is to be devoted to the Lord in both body and spirit. As a single and saved woman, your focus should be on God and doing His work, growing closer to Him, and enjoying yourself and your "peace of mind and not being focused on a piece." That's right!

Don't let your flesh force you into something you're not prepared for. Singleness is a gift from God.

Listen, Lindas, be content where you are. Enjoy you! Take yourself out and love on yourself, embrace your season of being single, have a solid sense of confidence in who you are and what makes you happy, pursue your goals, and be okay with spending time alone with yourself. If you don't want to spend time with yourself, then who do you think wants to spend time with you for the rest of their life. Use your time for preparation and to deal with the skeletons in your closet. You are single for a reason. What is in you that God wants to deal with before He allows your man to come? Learn yourself and be real with yourself. If you are purposed to get married, stay devoted to God, create a prayer life, find out what your spiritual gifts are, and begin to use them. Having the spiritual gift of discernment is essential. You need to be vigilant and sober-minded before he comes. Too often, we allow the flesh to rule and ignore signs that would have saved us from unnecessary pain. You need to be able to discern their motive. Why does he want to marry you? Is he broken looking for a fixer? Does he want to be nurtured? Is he looking for a mother instead of a wife? Is he looking for a business partner? Is he a lazy man looking for someone to support him? Is he abusive and looking for someone he can abuse? Or will he be the man that understands the importance of his rib? Those are things you should be able to discern, ask, and be okay with saying no and not right now, when you see the red flags. Even if that means you will have to be alone a little longer. Don't allow yourself to make a lifelong decision that you may regret.

We live in a time now when marriage is often viewed as a fairytale because of what is seen on social media and TV. Both are staged. And the real work starts after you take off the fairytale gown and cross the threshold. Marriage is solely designed for two individuals to become one flesh which means you MUST die to yourself to grow together. I believe if marriage is built correctly on the proper foundation, it can withstand any storm; however, that is if the two people are willing to fight for it continually. Unfortunately, we don't have enough people to be transparent about their marital troubles to help others survive in their marital distress; marriages do have "trouble," although everyone's journey will be different.

Those who marry will have troubles (special challenges) in this life (1 Corinthians 7:28). Once I found out that I was purposed to be married, and hear me, I was very content being single, and while I was waiting, I was properly preparing myself spiritually. I often found myself studying the Word (that taught me what to do in a covenant and how to be treated as a woman), fasting (how to crucify my flesh and get a spiritual breakthrough), praying (how to commune with God), and a lot of spiritual warfare (understanding my power and my God-given authority, how to choose my battle, and who my battle was against). Everything I learned was needed in my first year of marriage and afterward, especially spiritual warfare.

Our first year was definitely challenging. We were two strong-minded individuals, young and trying to embrace our new marriage and yet still trying to figure each other out. Let me dispel the truth on those who say that because you have been with someone for so long before marriage and may have lived with them, and you think everything will be the same once you get married. That is far from the truth. You will learn something every day different about the person you thought you knew. In the great words of my maternal grandmother, you will never know someone as well as you think you do. It would be safe to say this first year was the year I was emotionally and mentally wounded. I believe he came into the marriage holding on to the old Shonda and some of my old ways. What I mean by the old ways is the part of me that he loved that catered to his flesh (sexually), and because of that, it was hard for him to totally embrace who I had become as his helpmeet. I was no longer just the good sex partner; I was now there to help spiritually, physically, mentally, and emotionally in every area of his life. When someone comes into your life focused on why they are in your life and what they need you for, that is their mindset. They are usually focused on that, and only God can change that. They will have to be willing to adjust to the reasons they were sent into your life.

Make sure the last place someone left you will not be the place they find you. Whatever you do, let it be known and seen that the old you is no longer at that address. Who I was then is not who I was when I got married? Whenever the enemy sees growth, he hates that, and the war is on. Beware of those that will use you to hide their own personal struggles and bring that into your marriage. If you are one dealing with childhood sexual trauma, molestation, being raped, fondled, or dealing with unclean sexual spirits, it is not your spouse's job to cater to that or be punished for your past. That is something you should get healed from before marriage. Be also mindful that through your sexual activities, such as pornography and masturbation, and not to mention the sexual soul ties you have willingly brought into your marriage and have not been freed from, which have brought unwanted spirits into your bedroom. Know that lust (lasciviousness) has a powerful influence, and don't underestimate it. If thoughts and spirits are not cast down and out and you are not delivered and healed from it, it will cause trouble in paradise (home) because now you are looking for your spouse to fulfill the sexual appetite of legions (sexual partners) that you/they are still connected to. So now your spouse has to fight with you through your sexual addictions.

Sex is an intimate divine connection God created for one woman and one man. It is good, pleasurable, and honorable. Your past sexual fantasies with others should not enter your bedroom. Sex shouldn't be forced, done out of obligation, or made to feel like it has become a chore. When something becomes a chore, you can pick and choose when you want to do it, and eventually, you will start holding back on it because what was enjoyable and fun in the beginning has now become boring or less desirable. I will confess that I am guilty of holding back, and I had a reason. I can say most of the time if a woman is holding back, there are reasons, and some of them are legitimate reasons; she is feeling like she is being disrespected, not properly cared for, or it can be trust issues from being cheated on, abused, or she is trying to obtain attention through communication and not sex, she's angry, she's tired of having to juggle career, children, and household. Or, for some, it could be that she's allowed her anger to turn her into an emotional manipulator that will give her the power to control because she has been provoked (husbands are not to provoke their wives). Because of that, she chooses to use what's in her power to control? Whatever the reason may be, this is wrong! Manipulation of any kind is unhealthy in a relationship. I agree that this behavior is sinful and can open doors to more sin in a marriage. I also agree that it's a problem when sex becomes more important than you honoring and respecting the one God gave you to love. Men are to love their wives as Christ loves the church, just as women are to submit to their husbands. (I will pick back up on that submission word.) The Bible states that our body is not our own, and we should not deprive one another except by agreement for a limited time in prayer and fasting. We should then join again so that Satan will not tempt us because of a lack of self-control. It is written; we can't argue this, but whatever you do, don't use scripture to manipulate or demand sex or anything else that you desire to see your partner grow in. I will also say you should not get married solely because you want to spiritually legalize your sexual desires.

It is a well-known fact that men are wired differently and can easily turn off their feelings and do what they need to do. Women are not wired that way. They can't just push their emotions to the side and sweep things under the rug as if nothing has happened. They want to talk. As stated previously, there are reasons why they hold back (and this is for some men that may be holding back as well). Take the time to find this out and be willing to change for a healthy marriage and sex life. For all the fellas, if you want to get her in the bedroom, start with intimacy, connect with her emotionally, let her know she is desired and loved, touch her in the right spots, and the rest will be history. To all my sisters, I implore you - if these men are going over and beyond to please you and being doers of the Word by loving you as Christ loves the church, unconditionally giving himself up for you, and washing you in the Word, do what's right by them and be creative. Someone would love to be in your shoes. What you see as a burden, someone else will see as a blessing.

Apostle Paul admonishes the believers to put away old childish behavior, *"When I was a child, I spake as a child, I understood as a child, I thought as a child; but when I became a man, I put away childish things"* (1 Corinthians 13:11, KJV). You must be willing to grow. There are two major characteristics of a child that can be detrimental to a marriage.

1. Children are "selfish." They have a me-first attitude. Satisfy me, and you will get what you want.

2. Children have "Temper Tantrums," which are unpleasant and disruptive behaviors or emotional outbursts that often occur in response to "unmet needs or desires." They are unable to express their needs or control when they are frustrated, so they have adult tantrums.

When these two behaviors are displayed, selfishness and unmet needs are a recipe for disaster. No one wins! With that being said, when I got married, I found that some of my behavior had to change. Being the independent woman who grew up watching independent women thrive in unpleasant situations affected my life positively and negatively. Because of that, I handled what needed to be done in my home as a single woman. When I got married, I remember when something went wrong and it wasn't handled when I thought it should've been handled; given the time that was allowed to be fixed and wasn't, I would jump in and call the repairmen or take care of what I needed to. After all, we are the help! We won't let things go down on our watch. I was being somewhat territorial over what was mine. I wasn't fully ready to release what I had worked very hard to obtain as ours. And in heated disagreements with this mouth I had, I was definitely not a pushover, but I eventually had to learn how to shut up (a powerful lesson to learn in a marriage, it's a time to speak, and it's a time to refrain from speaking).

I would say things such as, "This is my house and my car." (I would advise you to purchase something together to avoid these "mine" conversations. Start fresh if you can.) I had no one to tell me it was okay to be independent but not to emasculate the man in doing so. Don't deprive him of his role or identity (especially if your mate is dealing with insecurity). A man wants to feel needed and "significant." He wants to be affirmed, probably more than you are willing to because, as women, we think, why should we celebrate what God commanded you to do. However, everyone wants to be acknowledged and told they are doing a good job.

I also share candidly with you that it's okay to be independent, resilient, and capable of getting things done. I strongly encourage you to go into your marriage with the table and some chairs (as boss ladies) with confidence and knowing who you are (and build together). I do believe that there are some men that can handle independent women. They are men who will create a safe place by making you feel secure and are not easily intimidated by your confidence, success, and independence. But don't let the spirit of independence disrupt the harmony of your home. When everyone knows their identity and position in the marriage, it's a safe haven, and there will be no room for intimidation or competition. The main goal is to keep the peace. When peace is obtained, it must be guarded. It's one of the most powerful assets to have in life and marriage.

I had accomplished a lot as a single woman. I had become a whole woman with many adult responsibilities and a mortgage and was doing my thing in my early twenties. As a married woman, my priorities (notice I said my) had changed. I was looking for "security" (a safe place). I wanted to be protected and secure, meaning if something happened and I couldn't work, I wanted to feel at peace knowing my bills would be paid and our lifestyle would not be altered, which is something every woman should want in a marriage. As much as I enjoyed having good sex, that was no longer at the top of my list. I thoroughly enjoyed it as a married woman and knowing that the bed is truly undefiled. I learned that sex is a gift from God, and like all His gifts, it can be distorted and abused if not used accordingly. It is said that sex is the number one reason marriages fail, and I refuse to believe that. I believe most marriages are failing because the order of God is not being implemented in the homes. For me, when implemented, these are things that I feel would make intimacy and lovemaking that much greater in a covenant: healthy communication, a priest that is your prayer partner not just willing to pray for you but pray with you, a visionary to build with, a protector, and a provider. It is so imperative to discuss your expectations before you get married and continue stating what they are inside your marriage when you see things shifting.

Unfortunately, if someone doesn't acknowledge the cracks in the relationship, they could easily think that the old behavior is okay and will work with something new, and it won't work. Just like you can't pour old wine into a new wineskin, you can't take old wounds and ways into new relationships. The old habits and wounds will keep feeding the battle.

You have to find better ways to communicate; communication creates better relationships, and through healthy relationships, pure intimacy is birthed. It's impossible to have one without the other. Whenever there is a lack of communication, you will draw the attention of unwanted serpents. In Genesis 2:15-17, 3:1-7, Adam and Eve show the importance of communication. They did not have good communication skills, and because of that, they both ended up disobeying God. When you have poor communication in relationships, it can quickly go bad and end marriages. Proper communication can cause you to take your eyes off yourself and hear the other party involved. Eve's first conversation was with the serpent. The lack of communication with her spouse led to the downfall of humanity. Like Adam and Eve, we lacked healthy communication. It led to arguments that eventually opened the door to serpents of confusion and chaos, which also can be other people and other voices that will speak louder than your spouse in your garden. When you allow other voices to speak louder than your mate's, your commitment and loyalty will be questioned, and out of it, disrespect, and emotional and verbal abuse can and will happen. Saying hurtful things to one another is the behavior that left us both wounded and emotionally drained-and at times, I felt as though that was my way of defending myself.

How do wounds start? Glad you asked. A wound occurs when you intentionally hurt someone mentally, physically, or emotionally through insult and or injury, stressing the individual out with the intent to break them down, hoping to leave them feeling helpless and powerless. When we find ourselves hurt, we should immediately address that hurt to get a proper understanding and not assume. "Pain demands attention!" It is so important to create a space for intentional communication, avoiding unmet expectations and unreasonable expectations. That will easily leave individuals wounded. We have to stop bringing childhood trauma and coping mechanisms into adult relationships, leaving others wounded because we want to continue to behave like a child. By doing so, our trauma will leave others wounded. Trauma left unchecked is unhealthy for the mind, body, and soul.

It is a guarantee that you will be wounded emotionally, physically, spiritually, and verbally by something or someone at some point in your life. If you haven't, it's coming. These wounds will eventually leave scars, and your scars will be an indication that you survived and that you are healed. You will see you have in you what's necessary to close the gap of your injury.

PEARLS OF WISDOM

- Always yield to the plan of the producer (God).

- Always look for the wisdom in your wound.

- Accept where you are; something greater will emerge. Know that God is sovereign; He is in control.

- Know that God causes and allows everything for a reason. Whatever you do, stay pure in the process.

Chapter 2

The Suffering Will Build Character

~

"And not only this, but [with joy] let us exult in our sufferings and rejoice in our hardships, knowing that hardship (distress, pressure, trouble) produces patient endurance; and endurance proven character (spiritual maturity); and proven character, hope and confident assurance [of eternal salvation]."

(Romans 5:3-4, AMP)

Some things in life are non-negotiable. It is not open for discussion, neither can it be modified to fit your terms of agreement. There will be some things in life you will have to struggle in and suffer through. When you suffer well, you will be able to help others to suffer well. God will give you the grace that's needed once you embrace your struggle and suffering season. In the previous chapter, I spoke on childhood trauma. Childhood wounds and trauma, once again, can affect the way we see ourselves, people in the world, and how we deal with relationships and life issues. One of the most traumatic things I see this younger generation dealing with is an overwhelming level of ("know it all") anxiety and depression because of their inability to handle life's struggles. Many of them feel entitled, as if someone owes them something, and most parents are guilty of this because you made them feel like they are and were the center of the world, and indeed they were the center of your world. However, as parents, it is also your job to teach and prepare them for a world that will not give them preferential treatment. Unfortunately, your sweet little angel of a child will be met with disappointments, failure, pain, and rejection. It is all a part of life's journey. It is indeed a disservice when we choose to shield and protect them from life lessons learned from struggling and suffering. You have to let them fail and fight through their own personal storms. Failure has never hurt anyone; they will appreciate life and success better. All successful people have experienced failure. They survived because they were determined to learn from their mistakes by changing their approach. All of my struggles and disappointments became life lessons and tools to teach and equip my daughter about life and how to break generational curses. If you don't like it, you do something positive about it, and because of that, she has been on platforms and done things that I only dreamed of doing as a kid. I had to prepare her for a world that would not be nice to her, but she could choose to thrive, live, and lead despite life's oppositions.

There are valuable gems in your struggle and your suffering. Your struggles are what give you meaning; they are what cause the changes in your life. It's all the confusion and chaos you grow up in or put yourself in. Your struggles are designed to bring out the creativity attached to the pain from the suffering. Your creativity is found in the struggle, and the suffering and the pain that you experience from it will produce the godly character that God is after. This will happen when you choose to change your perspective on how you see the struggle. They both play a significant role in your life. Through struggling and suffering, you get to experience life's transformations.

I witnessed what they both looked like firsthand growing up in the Ole Asheboro Street Community, also known as the "Dust Bowl," named after our community park that was so full of dirt, dust, and drugs. Needless to say, a lot of dirt went on in the dust bowl. Not the best environment! But one I would grow to appreciate; diamonds are normally found in some dirty places. I grew up in a two-bedroom house with no air and no cable and knew what government assistance was in all forms. I remember being so ashamed to go to the store with that book of food stamps growing up, but I enjoyed the food from it. As an only child and the oldest grandchild on both sides of my family, I knew that there was something different about me.

I was a dreamer, a leader at heart. I was loved by many and disliked by some growing up simply because I didn't mind expressing my thoughts. I was always taken care of, didn't lack much, but desired more, and was determined to be a generational curse breaker. I was the one who was called grown/fast and predicted to be the wild one with a lot of babies. All because they didn't understand that I was living my dream out loud by expressing who I would later become. (Be careful how you let others speak and label your child or yourself while you are becoming.) Don't let others' understanding of you hinder your truth of who you are becoming. Most dreamers are not understood because they will never conform to naysayers and unhealthy environments. They will always dream their way out. The many Barbie dolls that I had the privilege of styling as far as I can remember, my bold personality, the fake nails my mom would find in the bed, the excessive amount of makeup and costume jewelry I wore, the bold fashion statements I would adapt to, some by choice and others by default because I was so tall. They didn't have tall jeans back then, so I would have to cuff mine to create my fashion trend to keep from being picked on for wearing what we called then high waters. These were all the things I entertained myself with that kept me focused on my dream. I was determined not to remain stuck in the hood. And because I had this determination, I survived the labels, and even being fondled as a preteen that left me questioning myself. Was I really being grown, and is that what attracted him to do that to me? Later, I realized that his behavior had nothing to do with me but with his own internal struggles because I wasn't the only one he did this to. I had to learn to forgive him and not hold myself in contempt for his actions. You have to be careful not to allow the offense of others to take root and live within you. It feeds your attacker. Like many others, I was afraid to share this; I didn't share with my mom until I was older, and my dad definitely later out of the fear of them both, especially my daddy, harming or killing the individual. If you haven't been able to share with someone about being raped, molested, or fondled, please free yourself and share; even if you are one of those that mama and grandma told you, don't you ever tell because it will destroy our family. Grandma has gone on, and you are still in bondage. It's not fair to you; seek a therapist or someone you can trust and get free, so you can help someone as I hope I am helping you. I am somewhat of a daddy's girl, with quite a few ways alike. The fond memories I have as a little girl are forever etched in my heart, never to be replaced. My dad worked a lot when I was younger. I remember him staying beside us in a one-bedroom duplex, and I tried to make his closet my bedroom because I wanted to be with my dad and have my own room.

I always felt safe with my dad around. I also feared my dad because I knew he didn't play. For whatever reason, he was the one my teachers wanted to call to tell on me when I got in trouble (because they liked him, I believe). My dad was cool, a flashy dresser, and he loved luxury cars; all this still remains. He was the one who taught me how to shoot a gun, but he would only let me do it on the 4th of July. He was the first to let me behind a steering wheel illegally. He was the referee to one of my fights as a teenager, and yes, he told me, "I'm tired, I drove all the way over here, and you better whoop their butt" (which he said another word); I did just that. I also hated when he disciplined me and then wanted to take me for ice cream and food to smooth over what he did. If not Tasty Freeze, it was Monroe's. I must admit the food was good, and it was always excitement at both locations. I always wanted to remain angry and keep pouting after he disciplined me, but later his actions in doing so eventually taught me that discipline is necessary, and like God, he was chastising me because he loved me. The few whoopings I got indeed made me a better woman. I remember when my dad moved from beside us and later got married for the second time, I felt like I had lost my dad for a season, and I did. The feeling I had was so unexplainable. As a tween/teenager trying to make sense of it all, I later discovered it was the feeling of abandonment, as there are different forms of abandonment. You have emotional abandonment where parents and caretakers are there, but they are not emotionally involved. They downplay your emotions or are not present to engage with you to listen as you express your feelings. Then there is physical abandonment. It's when the physical conditions aren't met, such as a lack of supervision, essential things for a kid to thrive, clean clothing and shelter, etc. What did that look like for me? It was emotional and physical; I lacked the emotional support. He wasn't present like I wanted him to be to engage and listen to my feelings as I was entering a pivotal point in my life as a teenager. And I lacked the supervision of my daddy, which left me uncovered to some degree. A mother can never fill the void of a father's absence in the home, and that's my opinion. I will honestly say that this played a part in me dating an older guy who, by the way, treated me well while I was in high school. When my dad found out because one of his friends told on me, he was furious. But he was absent at this time. I share this because the consistent presence of a father is so vital in a daughter's life. It is her first male relationship, and his impact can cause damage or shape her future by assuring her that she's loved and that she will become that strong, confident woman that will not have to deal with self-esteem and self-image problems. Most importantly, his influence in her life will help her pick the right type of man and never need to be validated by anyone. I don't look for validation. I'm truly grateful that my dad validated me, and where he fell short, we were able to talk about those times when he should've been there and wasn't. I was able to forgive, heal, and laugh at some of the moments we shared. God is a restorer. It is imperative that you bring closure to childhood trauma by addressing the issues when you can. Forgive and even laugh together, letting the devil know he didn't win.

My mom was and still is such a classy, stylish, and humble lady. My first best friend, I believe every mother and daughter should have the relationship I had with her growing up. She wasn't perfect, but perfect for me. There was nothing I couldn't share with her. Her favorite words were "Do as I say, not as I do." And, of course, I did both.

(Remember, parents, you are to lead by example, all eyes are on you.) I wasn't that one that had to sneak a lot, she gave me enough rope in my life to explore, and when I hung myself with it, she was there to discipline me with so much love and wisdom. I never revisited some of those areas again simply because of the compassion she showed me in my disobedience. Growing up, I saw her make so many sacrifices for me as a kid, all while trying to enjoy her life as a young mom and making sure I always had and literally coming to blows for her child. I saw it with my own eyes. She didn't play about her daughter. I have seen my mom and grandmother both be legit "boss women" in their own right. Real boss women are not those that wear the expensive labels, drive nice cars, live in big houses, or have six figures in the bank. Real bosses are the ones that know how to handle life's adversities by making the struggles look easy. They know how to build from nothing. I believe it is in your struggle that you will find the greatest strength. I saw my mother help carry the weight of a household. I saw my five-footer, feisty, and didn't play grandmother, seemingly taking two fish and five loaves of bread and feeding us and others if needed, making sure my aunts and I, who grew up together like sisters, had hot meals when we got out of school and my mom a hot meal after work. I also saw her get up every morning, like it was a job, with a broom in her hand, sweeping and cleaning our house. Before we had a washing machine, she put our clothes in the bathtub and hung them on the clothesline, something this generation knows nothing about.

She watched kids for extra income, not limiting herself to the government help and child support when my grandfather sent it. Pause!!! What a boss! (B)uilt (O)n (S)upernatural (S)trength. "Thank You, Hot Dot" (the name I gave her) for showing me how to survive in tough seasons. She was also my personal alarm clock, hollering, "If you don't get up, you are going to miss that bus, and your momma isn't going to get me." She was my girl. I loved how she could hold our secrets. Work and school didn't work well for me. And I was not a morning person then or now. She understood her assignment. It hindered nothing. I became a proud honors graduate of Grimsley Sr. High School.

Seeing them both go through wasn't good, but it was necessary to see my mother struggle being a single parent. And seeing my grandmother suffer in silence from infidelity and adultery in her marriage which she stayed faithful to until the end. She coped with the pain through many nights of drinking and listening to her favorites, Teddy Pendergrass, Marvin Gaye, Gladys Knight, and Sam Cooke. She prophesied her change amid tears, and she did live to see her change come; the one that walked out on her was the same one God sent back broken to apologize. There were many sad nights, and though I wished I could've taken her pain away, I know that her pain and suffering were not in vain. I learned so much from her wounds, and the wisdom she gave will last me a lifetime. She was the first person I had ever heard say, "You will reap what you sow." Though she was not a frequent churchgoer, she quoted scripture that I didn't know then but do now. We weren't made to go to church in my household, but my mom allowed me to be a part of other individuals' lives who would introduce me to church.

My mom wasn't the parent that would easily allow me to stay overnight with people. She allowed me to stay with some people, but not many, and my dad's first wife was one of them. I still acknowledge her as my stepmom because of the love she has shown throughout my life. It takes a confident woman to allow another woman to be a part of her child's life, and I always admired this about my mother. I was a little girl going to church with her, and I remember a lot. One of my fond memories is her putting me into the Girl Scouts as a brownie at her and my dad's church. I also was able to experience what real deliverance looked like at her family church, seeing demons being cast out, bodies being healed, and the power of God in action. It was very scary to watch as a little girl, but what a powerful church it was in the "grove community." That seed that was sown later played a part in the deliverance ministry that I now love and walk in boldly. And then "The Pulliams," my childhood best friend's family that later became my family. They literally lived five minutes away. It was the place in the neighborhood where I would see the dynamics of a family. It was like staying with the Huxtables. They loved and treated me as their own. And I knew if I stayed there, I would have to go to church; it was a requirement, and my love for church grew. And not to mention, I loved my Ma Pulliam's cooking. My Pop Pulliam was amazingly gifted and talented. He played guitar and sang in the choir at church and was part of several quartet groups, and I often traveled with them on Saturdays and Sundays when he had to perform locally and in different cities in that white station wagon. Later, I would join the choir with my godsister, who can sing really well. I later joined the junior usher board because my paternal grandmother was on the usher board. It was so ironic that my paternal grandmother and maternal great-grandmother were all a part of the same church, along with several aunts. It's safe to say it was our family church, and it prepared me for who I was becoming.

Then there were times I wanted to get out of the hood to refocus, and I would call my other grandparents, who lived in Sedalia, NC, (they were like my mom and dad), to come and get me. I really had the best of both worlds, a well-balanced life that allowed me to see success and struggle. I clearly understand you can't have one without the other.

My paternal grandmother (my twin) was the business owner of Ethel's Sandwich Shop and Gas Station, where she served her community with love and the best soul food (my cooking skills came from her). I witnessed what entrepreneurship and a healthy partnership looked like firsthand. My Papa supported my grandmother's business as he worked his job and did his janitorial business on the side, in which I had the privileges of helping on some weekends. Sunday mornings were always exciting when I attended church with my grandparents. As previously mentioned, they were active and faithful in ministry as deacon and deaconess and on the usher board. I remember coming home from church, playing dress-up in her heels, pearls, and hats, helping her prepare dinner and setting the table for Sunday dinner with her real china, and eating together as my Papa blessed the table as the head of the household. Later I would run around on their two acres of land as night approached, trying to catch lightning bugs in jars as they gleaned with joy watching.

My Papa was my world. He was also another positive male figure who played a vital role in the woman I am today. I will never forget the one whooping I received from him on a Sunday morning. He always teased me by saying I was a quick learner because that was his only time having to discipline me. It was disheartening to find out he wasn't my biological Papa as a little girl, but blood couldn't have made us any closer; he loved me, and I loved him so much. He loved my grandmother, and I saw him cater to her. As perfect as they seemed to me, they even had their challenges but fought through them. The lessons that I learned in that household were so valuable; they sustained me in my most difficult seasons, knowing that I came from strong independent women who never quit when struggle presented itself. Every Ruth needs a Naomi in their life, and I was blessed with four of them, not to exclude my great grandparents. I gained so much knowledge and wisdom from them all.

So, the challenge occurred when it was time for me to walk out the wisdom learned from them, and indeed it was all needed and played a significant part in my story. Every pit stop made in my life growing up was necessary and a part of my purpose. Rule #1: Never judge someone by what you see and the success you see someone walking in. You never know what an individual has gone through. My childhood made me who I am, and I am not ashamed of any of it. It's how we deal with our childhood that will determine the power that our past has over us. Self-reflection will always be the conduit to healthy relationships. Everything I needed to survive was instilled in me, and because of that, I cannot settle for average.

I learned that suffering is a vital part of salvation. The Bible tells us we don't suffer like the world. Suffering with Christ leads to eternal gain. If we suffer, we also reign with Him: if we deny Him, He also will deny us (2 Timothy 2:12, KJV). The call to the Cross is tough, but the eternal gain is worth the temporary pain. To follow Christ is to "die" to ourselves. Jesus never guaranteed a life of pleasure absent of pain. In fact, He taught that pain is profitable! One man being wounded on the cross resulted in many being afforded the opportunity to benefit from salvation.

God allows and causes the struggle, suffering, and crushing to build character and add value! Yes, value. By the time He finishes with you, your stock goes up. If you do not believe, remember the process of the grape, diamond, olive, and seed. When grapes are crushed, they produce wine. Diamonds form under pressure. When pressed, olives release oil. Seeds grow in dark places and are placed in the dirt to grow. Whatever or whoever God has allowed to crush, apply pressure, press, or place you in an uncomfortable place to transform your life, He knows what He is doing. He wants to build your character and your capacity to endure pain. I remember an old saying, "What doesn't kill you will make you stronger."

I found this to be a very true saying. I've learned more from pain than I've learned from pleasure. Pleasure is temporary once obtained. Pain will leave you stronger. It makes you more resilient. Once you have experienced the pain, you will respect life and the newfound lessons from the pain. I am truly not here to glorify pain but to say it has a purpose and it will pay off. Did you hear me? It will pay off!

There was a season in my life when I felt like I was a track star, jumping hurdle after hurdle. Apostle Paul speaks about life as a race, and indeed it is. This race isn't given to the swift or the strong but to the one who endures to the end. I ran track briefly in middle school, and I watched those that jumped hurdles and was always intrigued. As a hurdler, I found out you must stay focused and stay in your assigned lane to run the race. Jumping hurdles requires flexibility and endurance. Regardless of how difficult and painful the obstacles may be, you must keep going and remain flexible.

Being flexible is saying, God I am willing to bend in whatever direction is necessary to jump this hurdle before me, knowing that God will give you the power, strength, and the ability to jump the hurdles that seem insurmountable. When obstacles are presented to you, you have the choice to face them and jump or to face them and quit. My choice was to face them and jump. I had to keep telling myself that if He graced me to jump the first one, I could surely jump the others. If He got you through that, He would surely get you through what lies ahead.

It honestly never seemed like I had enough space to jump between hurdles before the next hurdle came. Winded and wounded, trial after trial, sorrow after sorrow, I kept jumping-all the while, not visible to the eye and sometimes not feeling it. My spiritual endurance was being fueled, and my character was being developed. My goal was to get to the end of my painful season.

I had to choose to jump the hurdles set before me of fear, disappointment, rejection, betrayal, shame, self-pity, and even the loneliness I was beginning to feel inside my marriage. Believe it or not, you can be lonely in a marriage, and you can easily become a roommate to your spouse where you both are just existing. To get out of that place, you will have to discover the disconnect. It is said that almost a third, or 31% of married people, report being lonely. Most lonely people are depressed people, which isn't an easy thing to battle through but can be defeated. This indicates emotional abandonment, being consumed with what makes you happy and not being in tune with what makes the other person happy inside the marriage. This will ultimately lead to one feeling lonely. To avoid this, you must first find happiness within yourself and stay consistent and engaged with what matters to each other.

Consistency should be a practiced behavior in life, especially in your relationships. It can serve as an antibiotic for a wounded, lonely heart and soul. Consistency is just as important as communication and commitment. Consistency will keep out the spirit of doubt and leave no room to question your character. Being consistent is where true trust is developed.

I believe that the #1 thing that keeps us from being consistent in our relationships and achieving everyday life goals individually and with our partners is we become uninspired and lose interest and creativity. Have you ever heard someone say he/she doesn't do what they did when I first met them? When this happens, someone or both parties have lost interest and creativity. And when you lose interest, you will have to fight seemingly ten times harder to reignite the fire, which I believe can happen if both parties are willing to fight through it. If not, you may have to decide to move on, which is never easy.

Having to deal with the pain from this place and accepting the reality that it may not end the way you or I want it to will make you grow "bitter or better." You have to decide which "B" you will be. I wanted to be better! For me, but also for those I believed that God had me jumping the hurdles for. My pain taught me empathy so that I would have more love and compassion towards individuals experiencing the pain I went through. It gives you the right to say, "I understand." Stop saying you understand when you don't. Only empathy developed through pain can cause you to relate to others, and help talk someone off the cliff, which brings me to one of my favorite stories in the Bible about the fearless Abigail, who talked David off the cliff of destroying his destiny. Everybody needs an Abigail in their life that has the right temperament and godly character to address situations calmly when confronted with a hot-headed person.

You will find her story in 1 Samuel, chapter 25. Abigail was married to Nabal, whose name meant "foolish." He allowed his sinful nature to take control of his life. Nabal denied David's request for food and shelter and did not show benevolence to David as was shown to him. This bothered David, and he swore to kill him. His wife Abigail met him on the road, and she offered him wine, grain, meat, cluster raisins, and cakes of figs (verse 18). She also fell in front of his feet, asking for mercy on behalf of her husband, Nabal. She tells David as she falls at his feet and says: "Pardon your servant, my Lord, and let me speak to you; hear what your servant has to say. Please pay no attention, my Lord, to that wicked man Nabal. He is just like his name-his name means Fool, and folly goes with him" (verses 24- 25, NIV).

Immediately, you are able to witness the character of Christ displayed by Abigail. She doesn't hesitate to show meekness and kindness. She was putting her life on the line while her husband was clueless about what was happening; she stopped David from killing him. Imagine if her approach was as harsh as her foolish husband's; it would have truly ended differently. Abigail was a peacemaker whose words fitly spoken were like apples of gold in settings of silver (Proverbs 25:11, AMP).

But Abigail finds herself in a miserable marriage, unequally yoked with a heartless, self-centered man. (Single ladies don't get yoked with someone who doesn't have the same morals and values as you do.) A foolish man or woman will not know how to treat a king or a queen properly, so choose wisely. Getting involved with a foolish and selfish individual will cost you more than you are willing to pay. Abigail, who was not just beautiful but intelligent, walked in wisdom and had a deep respect for her husband despite his godless behavior. He blatantly said no to God instead of letting God have complete control over his life. And in doing so, it led to his premature death. When you choose to walk in disobedience willingly, please understand you open yourself up for death. God will bring you to the end of yourself, one way or another. You must continue to obey Him in dark seasons. Please believe He will and knows how to deal with your enemies. It is very obvious Nabal's arrogance stood in his way. I love how she was loyal to her husband but didn't condone or co-sign with his ungodly behavior. Never allow your loyalty to someone to cause you to be in agreement with their folly. Stop hindering people's growth because you are afraid to speak the truth about their behavior and fear losing the relationship. It will ultimately lead to their demise if they are not confronted with the truth. Her godly character saved her and the future king, who later became her husband.

God has predestined His people to be conformed to the image of His Son and display His character. Godly character is a prerequisite for being used by God. Embracing it helps to center our minds and lives around His Word. This will be necessary to finish the race.

After being stripped down to nothing, I lost everything but my mind, and sometimes I questioned if I wanted to continue to live through this painful fruit-bearing process, it was the Word of God that kept me. *"You have not chosen Me, but I have chosen you, and I have appointed and 'placed and purposefully planted you,' so that you would go and bear fruit and keep on bearing, and that your fruit will remain and be lasting, so that whatever you ask of the father in my name (as My representative) He may give to you."* (John 15:16, AMP). *"I am the Vine; you are the branches. The one who remains in Me and I in him bears much fruit, for (otherwise) apart from me (that is, cut off from vital union with Me) you can do nothing"* (John 15:5, AMP).

As the vine, His objective is not to keep us as we are. The only way we can become who He has called us to be is that we are willing to bear fruit, and until that fruit is evident, He will keep pruning us repeatedly, sending trials to mature us.

If we are going to make it through the trials and tribulations, we must remain, abide, and be in close proximity to Him. Apart from Him, we can do nothing. When we abide in Him, we submit our mouth, ways, will, choices, and decisions to Him. Lord Jesus! Help us. I promise this isn't easy, but it is worth it.

God is looking for the fruit that will remain and that gives an external action from an internal condition of the heart that can only be produced and cultivated by the Holy Spirit-being able to love the unlovable, loving that person that isn't easy to love, that one that may not have your best interest at heart. They may have mistreated, abused, rejected, abandoned, and disrespected you. Still, you choose to love them, in spite of. That's the fruit God is looking for. You do not know what I am talking about unless you know what it is to be in that place, where you want to hold on to the offense of the person who harmed you, and He won't let you stay there because your purpose depends on it. Because God is so rich in mercy, His love is everlasting. He keeps pruning and cleansing us, not to condemn us but to invoke a level of holiness that will inspire us to grow and give us the power to obtain victory over our flesh until He sees the fruit of love manifested. That love is unconditional and holds no wrong, the Agape Love of God; this love is not self-producing. It is a love that can only come from the source. By exemplifying this type of love, it's pleasing to God, and I found out that you are not required to be around the person[s]; but you can love them from afar and show them love while in their presence.

As we look at Galatians 5:22-23, we see the fruit of the spirit we should bear love, joy, peace, patience, kindness, goodness, gentleness, long suffering, and self-control. Once again, a branch must stay connected to the vine to grow and to stay alive. The purpose of the branch is to bear fruit that the vine produces, the fruit that have been tried and purified by fire, and that fruit will be evidence of Christ's work in us.

YOUR YES WILL COST

~

A wise person sits down and counts the cost. The word that every woman desires to say in her life after hearing "Will You Marry Me?" is "Yes." The thing most aren't prepared for is the cost you will have to pay for that yes. Paying for the wedding and the reception is small compared to the cost of the many sacrifices that will be made. The greatest One showed us that love really does cost. "For God so loved (Shonda) the world that He gave His only begotten son" (John 3:16, NKJV). Love costs, and walking with God will cost you, so sit down and see if you are willing to pay the price.

By saying "Yes" to God, I was relinquishing my will to Him, saying, "God, I love You," "God, I trust You," and "God, I will obey You." Exchanging my plans, desires, and ideas for His, I found out that saying "Yes" to God was and is the most painful yet rewarding choice I could have made. God will never force you to say yes; He is such a gentleman. He waits patiently for the yes because He knows He will eventually get the yes. Jesus' yes sounded like this, *"Nevertheless, not my will, but thine, be done"* (Luke 22:42, KJV). He said these words after realizing He couldn't pass the cup. There will be times you would like to pass the cup and throw in the towel because I did. Don't do it! Nothing will be wasted from this season of trials you may be experiencing.

When you do not say yes, you reject God's plan for your life. I get it. It is hard to say yes, not knowing what you are saying yes to. I said yes to marriage, not to the struggle or suffering I experienced, but it was all a part of it. Not knowing at that time, I was saying yes to my very own personal death. I am reminded by so many in the Word of God that said yes, and it cost them a lot. Like me, I am not sure if they counted the cost before they said yes. Noah said yes when told to build an ark. Abraham said yes when God asked him to sacrifice his son. Joseph said yes when God asked him to forgive his brothers. Job said yes when told to pray for his friends who falsely accused him. Esther said yes when asked by Mordecai to go before the King to save the Jews. They all suffered something in saying yes to Him, but they still gave a "Yes!" and the end was so rewarding.

CHAPTER 3

Don't Abort The Process

~

"Trust in the LORD with all thine heart; and lean not unto thine own understanding."

(Proverbs 3:5, KJV)

Have you ever had a hard time trusting someone? Have you ever heard someone tell you to "trust God?" I must admit I am not one who can easily put my trust in an individual. I will also be the first to tell you that trusting God is not an easy thing to do when you are in a difficult season. Trusting in God doesn't mean you will get your way, and your process will go the way you want it to. How can you trust someone you have never seen or had to build a relationship with? Let's look at the definition of trust. According to Webster, trust is an assured reliance on the character, ability, strength, or truth of someone or something; a person or a thing in which confidence is placed, a dependence on something, having hope in someone.

In order to trust in someone, it will require work on your part. You will have to build a genuine relationship with that person in order to place your confidence and hope in them. God allowing you to go through a process is the assurance that you will gain trust in His character, ability, strength, and His truth. And there is no other way that this can be done unless you willingly go and grow through a process. Doing so will allow you to build a relationship with Him, knowing that He has your best interest in mind. I am reminded again by one of my favorite books in the Bible, none other than the book of Job (by the way, I am his twin Job-a-Lina). In Job 1:1, there was a man who lived in the land of Uz whose name was Job; and that man was blameless and upright, and one who feared God (with reverence) and abstained from evil (because he honored God). News flash!! Because you honor someone doesn't mean you trust them. Job was a man who honored God, but he hadn't developed a relationship to trust Him.

In verses six through eight, it gets interesting. *"There was a day when the sons of God (angels) came to present themselves before the Lord, and Satan (adversary, accuser) also came among them. The Lord said to Satan, 'From where have you come?' Then Satan answered the Lord, 'I have been patrolling the earth, watching everything that's going on.' The Lord said to Satan, 'Have you noticed my servant, Job?'* (Insert your name where Job's name is.) *For there is none like him on the earth, he is blameless a man of complete integrity, one who fears God [with reverence] and abstains from and turns away from evil [because he honors God]."* In verse 12: *"Then the Lord said to Satan, Behold, all that Job has is in your power, only do not put your hand on the man himself. So, Satan departed from the presence of the Lord."* Here you see Job's process was approved by God, and this process opened the eyes of Job about material things. *"The Lord gave and the Lord taketh away; Blessed be the name of the Lord."*

God is not concerned about your material things in the process. He knows He can replace those things but what He is concerned about is you getting to know Him on a personal level. Your initial reaction to your process indicates how well you know the God of the process. Job's process was so intense his wife said to him to curse God and die. She was basically saying to him, "abort your process, give up." Be careful who you listen to when you are in your process. Although her advice wasn't right, it was a normal response to someone who leans to their own understanding. His response to her was you speak as one of the "foolish women" speaks (ignorant and oblivious to God's will). Shall we indeed accept (only) good from God and not also accept adversity and disaster? Despite all this, Job did not sin with words from his lips. While in your process, you must learn to speak well of the God of the process. The last point I would like to make concerning this scene is a divine setup by Him. In Chapter 42:5-6, Job makes a confession that says, "I had only heard rumors about you before, now I have seen you with my own eyes." Job had a face-to-face encounter with God. The process is designed for you to see the man in the mirror (you). Through his confession and repentance, he began to see that he had become a broken and a changed man. When we say we really see God, we should see brokenness and change. He is looking for us to trust Him like a child. This type of trust will be developed only through humility. Our future is in the hands of God. We must trust Him with the timing and the fulfillment of our promise. I will admit the crushing process is very painful. But it is also rewarding. If you can shift your focus off of you and the woe is me attitude and on the promise, it makes the process a little easier to bear. As I think of the word "bear," we are called to bear the pain as a woman in labor.

At the age of 40, I went through one of the most traumatic, painful, and humbling seasons of my life, bearing the pain of a miscarriage. The pain from that was emotionally, physically, and mentally draining. There was a roller coaster of emotions such as, but not limited to, emptiness, depression, grief, failure, and guilt. I thought this was really my breaking point. It's over. I had dealt with so much before this: the foreclosure, bankruptcy, repossessions, a dysfunctional marriage, and now bearing the pain of losing a child at six months pregnant. This miscarriage left me empty and disappointed. It was an unplanned pregnancy, but a pregnancy I would gain some hope in believing would be what would bring my husband and me closer.

Unfortunately, it was not, and I felt that I had nothing else to lose at this point in my life. I really thought I was Job's twin. It seemed as though I had lost everything he lost. Carrying the weight of marriage, the responsibility of ministry, and the pain of my miscarriage had certainly become more than I wanted to bear.

Being a mother to my daughter was an additional responsibility. She is what kept me in my fight a little longer. It is very important to have a why when going through your process and my why brought me so much joy and fulfillment. Our mother and daughter bond is genuinely perfect. She was indeed what I needed to survive. By giving birth to her, I found out that God will still bless you in a mess. I call to remembrance that my faith was being challenged after giving birth to her. She was a preemie (born early), which resulted in her going to NICU (Neonatal Intensive Care Unit) for a short while. The enemy was after her and didn't succeed. I am fully persuaded that no one but God got me through this tough season that I could have never imagined myself going through. Every storm will pass over! Though destructive, at times, they will not last forever. It is said that God gives the hardest tests to the strongest soldiers, and He will never give you more than you can bear. You will begin to question all of that when the load seems too heavy to carry. Also, during this time, I was a caregiver, Power of Attorney, and Executor of Estate for my maternal and paternal grandparents, a position I didn't ask for but a position that God saw fit for me to be in. Being a caregiver comes with emotional, mental, and physical stress. They all started passing, seemingly right after each other. By this time, I had become immune to losses.

The weight was heavy! I felt as though I didn't have another tear to cry. I had become numb. This is when the enemy will come at your lowest points, talking to you, telling you to give up, throw in the towel, go back to familiar behavior, or do things you have never done to ease the pain. This is when you can easily start slipping, being married but having an affair on the side, you start back drinking, doing something foolish to get back to the one who inflicted the pain. Absolutely not. In God's timing He will vindicate you for all the pain you endured. You and your name will be restored. Vengeance is mine; I will repay, saith the Lord. Never avenge yourselves.

This type of behavior only affects you. So absolutely not! When you mean business with the Lord, you put away all the games believing that the God you serve will vindicate you and bring you out. I was determined to come out with clean hands and a pure heart. For me, this was when I had to grab the horns of the altar tighter and allow God to continue to get rid of everything that didn't please Him and fight to get to my breakthrough. I found that peace and my greatest strength came through much prayer, praise, staying in His Word, and worship.

When you're going through fiery trials, it is so important to keep a song on your lips and an encouraging word in your heart. David said it best in his distress; he had to learn to encourage himself in the Lord. And if you're going to survive your places of hardship, you must do likewise. One of the ways I had to encourage myself was through a familiar story that I learned as a child, *The Little Engine That Could*. Her famous line was, "I think I can, I think I can." In your darkest hours, you must find something to hold on to. Say this out loud, "I think I can. I know I can."

You can get through whatever you're going through if you change your perspective. If you can remember the story, the little blue engine was smaller than the other trains. She had never been over the mountain and was less experienced than the other trains. But what I loved about her was that she believed in herself and her ability to do what seemed impossible. She didn't allow the spirit of comparison to steal her moment. Her focus wasn't on the other trains. I can recall going through my trials. I occasionally looked at someone else's journey and relationship, comparing it to mine, because it seemed like they weren't having problems. Whatever you do, don't allow the spirit of comparison to steal the uniqueness of your journey or relationship. Comparison is the thief of joy that can lead to competition, which opens the door to envy. That's why it's so important to know who you are and have faith to believe that you will make it up the hill no matter how heavy your load is. Regardless of how impossible the task may seem, your valley experience will equip you with what you need to help yourself and someone else. What's on your load? Whether it's childhood trauma from your past, adulthood drama, abandonment, betrayal, abuse, molestation, rape, being fondled, rejection, disappointment, church hurt, sickness, divorce, separation, financial hardship, job loss, or loss of loved ones, you will get through it. You will heal if you do not keep picking at the scab and rehearsing the pain. I am living proof. You must remember this is not for you; this is for someone else.

The wound that caused so much pain will become a memory; you will see the scar and will not feel the pain. I have some scars on my body that I can laugh at, remembering how I got them, and some scars I do not see, but I can remember the pain.

Be assured God will not waste anything you go through. He doesn't make mistakes. He uses the process to authenticate you. Imagine if Jesus had aborted His process. He understood the assignment and knew that it would be something greater that would emerge from His process, you and me. Don't you quit! Be determined to continue to fight and not faint. Something good is coming out of this. Psalm 147:3, KJV declares, *"He is a healer of the broken-hearted."* He is the One who bandages their wounds. That is a promise; He will heal your brokenness and bring all your broken pieces back together again. Though it seems lonely as you travel this road, God is there with you as He was with me. Don't come out of the fire too soon. Those God has assigned you to need you delivered, healed, and whole.

> *"The steps of a good man are ordered by the Lord, and he delights in his way and blesses his path"* (Psalm 37:23, KJV).

> *"Be sober (well balanced and self-disciplined), be alert and cautious at all times. That enemy of yours, the*

> *devil, prowls around like a roaring lion, fierce and hungry, seeking someone to devour but resist him be firm in your faith against his attack (rooted, established, immovable), knowing that the same experiences of suffering are being experienced by your brothers and sisters throughout the world (you do not suffer alone)* (1 Peter 5:8-9, AMP).

YOU ARE NOT SUFFERING ALONE

~

Beloved, you are not suffering alone! Far from the truth, as stated previously, everyone will suffer something at some point in their life. I remember feeling alone and alienated, not having many to talk to because it appeared as though everyone had a perfect marriage in the church. So, it left me feeling like an outcast, so I suffered in silence for a season-the danger in doing that will open the door to depression. And for me, I closed that door quickly by acknowledging and exposing it. To suffer in silence brings more pain which leads to more trauma. Being transparent and approachable will help others open up to you when suffering. I honestly believe that's why we see a surge in suicide and mental health issues. People will isolate themselves, hide their truth and refuse the help they need for fear of being judged or showing their vulnerability. When you suffer, the best way not to feel alone is to open up, speak up, embrace it, and own it, believing that God will send people and the comforter (Holy Spirit) to comfort and strengthen your faith to endure and He will also be with you, never leaving or forsaking you. Suffering is only for a little while. Your willingness to submit and change your perspective can change how long you suffer and how long you stay in your cave.

David, who was a man after God's own heart, a fugitive running from Saul, found himself in a cave alone but not lonely. He was being prepared for something much bigger than the suffering he was experiencing. He needed protection in a dark season of his life. Sometimes, your protection will be found in a cave. There are lessons to be learned in the cave. David learned how to behave and be patient in the cave while waiting on God's timing to become king. God never intends for you to stay in the cave. It is not a permanent place. It's your training ground and for you to help others. David trained others while he was in the cave. In my personal experience, I found that caves allow you to be you! Caves are where you can be naked and not ashamed with God; it's a judge-free zone where you can share your heart with Him. It's the place where transformation takes place. The Bible states that David became greater because the Lord was with him. Even at his worse, God used him to help someone else become better.

I believe that God is raising and releasing a remnant of cavemen and cavewomen that have been prophetically set apart. You will come out of your prophetic delay anointed and properly aligned, and in agreement with heaven's plans and the purpose for your life. Some of you feel this uncomfortable adjustment because you have gotten so used to poor spiritual posture (living how you want to live, doing what you want to do). And you can't do this when God has called you. If you have ever gone to a chiropractor before, you know they focus on misalignments of the spine. When the spine is not in alignment, it blocks communication between the central nervous system and the rest of the body, and when that happens, it can cause other health issues. When the adjustments are made, it will restore your alignment and give you proper function and movement to your joints and spine. When God (the chiropractor) does a spiritual alignment on you, He focuses on the misalignments as well. He desires to restore proper communication and make you mature enough to function in the capacity in which He is calling you so that others are delivered, healed, saved, and trained through your willingness to conform to the will of God in an uncomfortable situation. God deliberately ordered this defining moment in your life to humble you before He elevates you. If you stick to His treatment, you will see that the alignments will work, and they are necessary. Our lives, hearts, and minds can easily get out of alignment with the will of God for our lives, and when this happens, we must take an honest assessment of our own lives. David had to give an account for his own sin. The moment he did that, he began to grow, and from that growth, he became king. To make those adjustments, the GPS (God Positioning System) has to reroute us and realign us.

I can recall saying, "Lord, like David, I need a 'Cave of Adullam (a place of refuge),'" and I found my cave at the Embassy International Church, not knowing they had a ministry in place called "The Cave" for ministers and pastors. You see how God already had me in mind. Before I got there, He had ordered my steps and had prepared a place for me, not knowing that my pastor would be the same man that sold me "hair products" for my business years ago.

God is so strategic. It was the place where I was rebuked, challenged to grow, and allowed to heal. I was able to dream and hope again. My anointing was respected and protected, not prostituted. You have to have accountability while in the cave. If you're going to be who God has called you to be, you have to be accountable to somebody. You will not successfully get to that destination alone. Don't avoid your cave experiences; your cave is your recovery room. It's the place where you will be closely monitored and fully woke before you are released into your divine assignment. Had David not been provoked to run from Saul, he wouldn't have experienced the cave. There are times that God will orchestrate chaos to get us to where we need to be.

Just because you run from something, or someone doesn't make you a coward. When God is in it, a retreat is a blessing. David had reasons to run! And so did I. Deciding to run from my church then as First Lady/Co-Pastor was one of the hardest decisions I had to make. There comes a time in your life when you have to make decisions that may hurt and offend others but will ultimately save your life. It was my walk of shame, and yes, I was very ashamed and hurt that I had to leave some of my spiritual babies and take my daughter away from what was our normal.

Whenever you start losing respect, or you wrongly become a threat to who God has placed in authority, the best thing for you to do is "RUN" for the sake of getting in trouble with God and compromising your integrity. David found himself running from Saul, a strong leader and warrior, a man who allowed himself, through the spirit of pride, fear, insecurity, jealousy, and anger, to lose control and cause his own destruction. The very one he thought he was in agreement with him was the one that was seeking to destroy him. *"How can two people walk together except they agree?"* (Amos 3:3, KJV). When agreement leaves, God leaves. There is power in agreement, favor is bestowed upon agreement, and lastly, you are guaranteed victory when you agree. *"Where two or three are gathered in my name, I am in the midst of them"* (Matthew 18:20, KJV).

It is imperative that you learn the lessons in your trial; if not, you will repeatedly go through the same cycle with the same person, another person, or another situation. My process was tailor-made for me as your process is tailor-made for you. God knew what it would take to break me. Just like He knows what it will take to break you. He's intentional about the breaking process; He breaks to position and promote us. He knows everything, and nothing is ever hidden from Him. He knows all the secrets, sin, and hurt we tend to hide. Nothing in all creation is hidden from God. Everything is naked and exposed before His eyes, and He is the one to whom we are accountable (Hebrews 4:13, NLT).

David was being exposed to set him free from old behavior. The old saying is you can take the boy out of the hood, but you can't take the hood out of the boy. His cave was designed to get the hood out of him (David had game and was from the hood, I don't care what ya'll say). God wanted him inwardly clean and protected. Be assured that He is protecting you. Amazingly, everybody can't go with you, and everybody can't handle your process.

Johnathan was David's close friend who helped him against his controlling and manipulative father, but he couldn't get into his process. In fact, his presence endangered others. Do not invite someone into your process, and do not voluntarily get into anyone else's process unless you are led to because you will definitely have unjust suffering. What do I mean by that? If you get into a relationship with someone who hasn't been healed from past trauma, they will bring drama into your friendship or relationship, and you will find yourself being everything but what the connection was purposed for. If your significant other has mommy/daddy issues, they are coming into the relationship looking for a mother to nurture and a daddy to validate them. That person will require a lot of attention, seeking approval and looking for someone to always agree with them, and when you don't, they will feel like you are against them. Seeking validation disempowers us from living our own life. Anxiety and depression will begin to play a part when we don't get enough validation from others. Seeking validation will also keep you disconnected from following your own heart. You will find yourself living for others.

So do yourself a favor and get healed before you marry someone. Don't include them in your process. It's unfair to them. And it's not fun! Have you ever got a whooping that was not for you? But you got it because you were with someone it was intended for. Your wounds are yours. They will help you draw closer to the Lord, but your scars will be help for others. Endure your process, maintain your posture, and be steadfast and unmovable. He is molding you into His masterpiece that He will use for His glory. **Do not abandon or abort the process!**

CHAPTER 4

Remodeled For Purpose

~

"For we are His workmanship [His own master work, a work of art], created in Christ Jesus reborn from above-spiritually transformed, renewed, ready to be used for good works."

(Ephesians 2:10, AMP)

I can recall getting my first apartment when I was 19 years old. Everything I had in that apartment was nice to me. My furnishings were current for the time. For those that can remember, in the early '90s, everyone had the black and white marble, brass-trimmed bedroom set. Lol! I was living my best life! You could not tell me anything. On my own, my own bedroom, no longer having to share a room, I was finally free. I loved everything about turning that key to my own place. I knew that wasn't the end, only the beginning. My goal was to own my own home. Well, at the age of 21 (the first to do it at my age in my immediate family), I purchased a three-level townhome. It needed to be remodeled badly. It needed to be brought up to date. I wanted the look of my townhome to reflect who I had become. But that wasn't going to happen without a process.

HGTV became my favorite show to watch for ideas; I became fascinated by how outdated homes and old furniture could be transformed into something new.

As I began to observe what needed to go and be changed in my place, the green carpet was the first thing that had to go. I hated it because it was dirty, ugly, and outdated. The carpet was immediately ripped away; it was the beginning of months of my remodeling process for the home. I quickly discovered the cosmetic part would be the easy part of the renovating and remodeling process. I learned when you are cosmetically changing things, you are improving the appearance of a person or a thing. You're changing it aesthetically and not focusing on the useful purpose, and by doing this it will do nothing to help the situation long-term. I was changing the appearance of the flooring but wasn't focused on the foundation of the flooring. The damage that was obvious to the contractor wasn't obvious to me; my only concern was the appearance. Sadly, most of us are more concerned about our outer appearance than we should be, and it doesn't help our long-term growth. Social media has changed the way we see ourselves, so we are constantly changing our appearance to keep a certain image to cover up internal wounds by adorning ourselves to look good externally while overlooking what needs to be changed internally.

When God takes us through a process to remodel us, He wants to change our internal condition. He gives us our own personal HGTV episode of (How God Transforms Vessels). He desires to rewire us because internally, we can look like that carpet, dirty and outdated. So, He will use people and situations to expose all the faulty wiring in our hearts that we have built walls around. The signs of faulty wiring are dimming or flickering lights (sin and pain dims our light), blowing breakers or fuses (attitude), showing no self-control, and being easily triggered from past trauma (you go from zero to a hundred). And if this is not corrected, it can cause unwanted fires in relationships. He wants to cut out and rip away all the outdated, damaged, poorly installed thoughts and old behavior.

Though the remodeling process can be long and grimy, the results are always something beautiful in the end. God has to break us down to the foundation to rebuild us and rewire us to fulfill His purpose and plan for us. A breakdown is always needed for a breakthrough. A quick fix will never work for the master contractor.

We must stop trying to be our own contractor, trying to fix ourselves and allowing the enemy to play games with our minds, knowing that the devil's desire is for us to stay stuck, never maturing as the men and women that God has called us to be. We must stop constantly making excuses by saying things like: "This is just how I am," "I'm fine like I am," or the famous "I am human." I will agree that we are, and we deserve a human card pass every once in a while, but don't keep using it to justify your need to stay the same. It will prolong your remodeling process. Relinquish your rights and control and admit that you are flawed clay and need Him to reshape and mold you into the vessel that He desires to see. He knows what He wants the final product to look like. That's why He is the master contractor. Remember He sees in you what you don't see in yourself!

I remember some of the annoying times in the remodeling stages of getting my townhome completed. I was living in the mess while the contractors were in it doing the necessary makeover. I had to learn how to still function in my home as it was being remodeled. This reminded me of how I bled internally while functioning as a wife, mother, daughter, granddaughter, friend, First Lady/Co-Pastor, and entrepreneur. The functions don't change or stop because you are being remodeled. You are still who God called you to be; you just have to live in the mess until He makes you over. I was on the road to perfection (maturity). I had to limp until I learned. I bled till I bowed. With this said, I wore my hardship as a badge of honor, not looking like what I was going through. As polished as I looked on the outside, I was broken on the inside, longing for my remodeling process to be over.

I was tired, sick and tired of dealing with loss after loss, betrayal, and being assassinated by people I thought should have loved me and had my back as I had theirs. It's a painful thing to be connected to people you can't trust. On this journey, I've learned so much about God. He can always be trusted, you can't curse what He has blessed, and He doesn't do anything halfway. He takes pride in what He does. And what He does will come with a lifetime warranty that will stand the test of time. Although it may be painful, it will produce a harvest of righteousness.

"No discipline seems pleasant at the time, but painful. Later on, however, it produces a harvest of righteousness and peace for those who have been trained by it" (Hebrews 12:11, NIV). To be trained through hardship can be the most daunting thing, but the truth of the matter is that hardships have great benefits for our growth. Without it, we will stay stagnant and stay in sin. With that said, you can easily think you have matured in the place that God is still disciplining you in. He will send another test right when you thought you were on your way to recovery. He sends the test to keep you in pursuit of Him, and He watches to see if you will allow your emotions to hinder your commitment.

You must watch your emotions in your healing process. Your emotions can easily cause you to start picking at the scabs that are starting to cover the wound. You start rehearsing the pain. When you start doing this, you are setting yourself up for a setback, which leads to self-sabotage (behaviors or thought patterns that can hold you back and prevent you from doing right and moving toward your goals and healing). You have to get out of your own way. You're hindering your healing. You are worthy of the freedom and the harvest that is waiting on your arrival.

So, as you begin to heal, avoid being the emotional scab picker at your soul wounds in the remodeling process. Going through my very own process, I was a scab picker, constantly going back and forth and revisiting the same things with no change. The danger in picking at the scab is that you will keep yourself in repeated cycles and on emotional roller coasters by pointing fingers (the blame game), constantly revisiting the place of pain, seeking revenge, and being frustrated and angry behind the wound. Doing this can keep you in a wounded place longer. Let God form an invisible scab to protect your heart from further damage.

When you do this, you will experience His grace. The scab represents God's grace, the grace that can heal all wounds. The gift of grace that gives you compassion towards others while He continues to transform you into His image; it is the grace that covers and gives you what you don't deserve. It is the grace that gives you the strength to live from day to day. When I finally discovered this grace, it was a gold mine. In this part of my journey, I finally gained some strength and started to understand why I was being remodeled and rewired mentally and why He allowed Satan to come and test me in the areas

I needed the most. My newfound grace made it easier to accept what God had allowed.

I had to learn what spiritual self-care looks like and how to apply the Word in my test and walk by faith and not by sight. I promise you this was the hardest thing for me to do.

I didn't need faith when I had money, good health, and good credit. It wasn't until I was stripped of everything that I had to learn how to develop my faith. If you are in this place of developing your faith, please look up to the hills from where your help comes from. Stay focused on "JESUS," the author and the finisher of your faith and His word. Also, hang around people that live by and walk by it. The more we develop our faith, the more we please God. Being tested on living a life that loves unconditionally and forgives with no hesitation is a very, very hard place. I didn't want to love and forgive him or those who had betrayed, abandoned, rejected, and mishandled me. It was easy and comfortable for me to stay in that place, but it wasn't beneficial to my growth. Forgiveness isn't for them that hurt you, but for you. It isn't condoning the behavior of the individuals, but it is accepting the reality of what happened and living with it. I had to willingly submit and continue to trust the Master Contractor to remodel me. When we willingly submit to our healing process, we will minimize the pain.

Once again, He knows the changes that are needed!

In mentioning submission, submission is not subjection, forced control, or dictatorship. Submission is not being robbed of your identity once you get married. God created you as an individual with your own purpose and journey. So many women lose themselves in marriages taking on the identity of their spouse. When you do this, ladies, you will rob yourself of fulfilling your purpose and being your authentic self. Know who you are, know how you are to be treated, and never allow anyone to make you second guess that. I honestly hated to hear the word submit sometimes because it was often used in error in the church and out of the church by those who wanted to control and exert power over others by breaking down a person's will. This type of submission is not of God. Submission was not just given to the woman. Submission is learning how to *"submit one to another out of the reverence for Christ, serving one another humbly in love"* (Ephesians 5:21, ESV). Submission is the act of someone who willingly yields to someone else's authority, in the home, in the church, on the job, and to government officials, etc. In marriage, submission is not one-sided; submission is respect and love. Wives are to submit to their husband's leadership, following them as they follow Christ. (Something that men fail to understand is that most women don't mind submitting as long as he is following Christ and leading her somewhere.) This doesn't mean that she is anything less than the man; they are co-equals and co-heirs in Christ. As Jesus is submitted to the Father, husbands should submit to the Father and love the wife as Christ loves the church.

Building the kingdom of God together requires submission. However, the religious gender roles and responsibilities that we try to enforce on one another in marriages can sow seeds of resentment and anger causing the marriage to suffer. You would be surprised at how many times in counseling sessions I hear men complain about the wife cooking and cleaning. Household responsibilities can be shared when serving one another is truly understood. Responsibilities are not gender-driven but Christ-driven. Don't allow the small foxes that can spoil the vine cause you to overlook the real value. Sometimes it is the little things that can cause the biggest problems. So much energy and time are focused on religious roles and self-pleasure that we drain ourselves mentally and emotionally and become useless builders because we neglect to follow the kingdom blueprint for the marriage.

God has a specific kingdom vision when He joins a man and a woman in holy matrimony. That vision must be carried out, with both parties willingly submitting to it. The vision is often given to the man. He is the temperature setter in the home, understanding if he wants respect, he must give it. If he wants to be honored, he must show honor. He sets the climate by cultivating peace and unity within the relationship. Men should take the time to understand what brings their (favor) partner joy and pain, for she is the one who maintains the temperature in the home. By doing so, you create a climate that will create a peaceful atmosphere and will ignite levels of intimacy. Resolving conflict will always create intimacy. Following God's blueprint for marriage to the best of your ability will always result in a win.

Marrying a man without a vision is a no-no ladies. Where is he leading you? When dating, once again, that is data that should be collected. And if your spouse doesn't know the vision and you are married, pray together, asking God for the purpose of your marriage, seeing that it is carried through by God's expectations. Wives, don't be bullies forcing it but have the patience to see if he will carry it through. Remember you married him without one. And for those with a vision and the headship is not implementing it the way God gave it or is not including you and has made it all about him, a one-man show, it's a disaster waiting to happen.

Speaking previously on Abigail and David, they both submitted to each other as brother and sister in Christ and aligned their will to God's will, and the conflict was resolved. They had one common goal: displaying a godly character that resulted in the purpose of God being fulfilled. David's vision was far greater than the animosity and food; he was getting ready to destroy his entire future behind a fool. Be careful not to fall into traps with destiny killers. Nabal submitted to no one; he was a fool and harsh in his dealings. His life is a reminder that:

- ❖ We will reap what we sow. Living a life that pleases God is vital.

- ❖ We must be careful how we treat individuals that we think are beneath us. When it's in your power to help, help!

- ❖ Respect and honor those that God sends us.

- ❖ Know that every action has a reaction.

He mistreated a future king, which could've been a setup for his advancement. Father, help us recognize the ones you send into our lives to help us become better so that we will not fight against them but understand the reason and purpose they were sent. Going through the remodeling process will help you get rid of the clutter and weed out the placebos in your life, and you will find out the ones who are for you and against you. Guarding your heart and space will be necessary as you advance towards becoming a better you. Learn to be okay with people talking. Let them doubt while God develops you. "Pigs will never understand the value of pearls."

> *"But He knows the way that I take (and He pays attention to it). When He has tried me, I will come forth as (refined) gold (pure and luminous)."* (Job 23:10, AMP).

> *"Your faith will be like gold that has been tested in fire. And these trials will prove that your faith is worth much more than gold that can be destroyed. They will show that you will be given praise and honor and glory when Jesus Christ returns."* (1 Peter 1:7, CEV).

> *"Behold, I have refined you, but not as silver; I have tried you in the furnace of affliction."* (Isaiah 48:10, ESV).

Pray this prayer: Father God, I submit to Your will. Change me, God, make me more like You, remodel me in the furnace of affliction. You are the potter; I am the clay. Mold me and shape me. Create in me a clean heart, O God, and renew a right spirit within me. Cast me not away from thy presence. Help me to shut the doors of my past and keep open the doors of my heart so that I may learn of Your ways as You rebuild this temple according to Your blueprint, Your plans, and Your purpose for my life. I will rejoice in knowing that You are with me and will never forsake me. In Jesus' name!

> *"Therefore, if any man be in Christ, he is a new creature: old things are passed away; behold, all things are become new."* (2 Corinthians 5:17, KJV)

CHAPTER 5

It's Time for a Reset

~

"After you have suffered for a little while, the God of all grace (who imparts His blessing and favor), who called you to His own eternal glory in Christ, will Himself complete, confirm, strengthen, and establish you (making you what you ought to be)."

(1 Peter 5:10, AMP)

A divine reset is a time that is predestined-the Kairos timing of God, the "opportune moment," the appropriate time, the right season. A new start. Your divine reset is designed to alleviate stress from life's wounds by rebooting the hardware (you) and bringing you into a place of wholeness. In the reset, it's not that you have lost power; you have lost your ability to function in the power. With the reset, you get another chance to get reacquainted with the existing power; it helps you to have a clearer focus on your purpose and His promises. Your suffering was not in vain. God has always been in tune with your condition. You can no longer focus on the coulda, shoulda, woulda. You can no longer allow the pain from your past to dictate your future. Every disruption in your life will bring about a divine reset. Your reset will delete, cancel, and clear your hard drive (mindset). He wants all the files of your past pain, failures, and trauma cleared so that you may function properly in your next season.

There was no way I could get a reset or hit the reset button without action on my part. This is probably where I'm getting ready to lose some of you. You're going to have to participate in your own reset (healing). Being healed will require you to take an honest inventory of the role you played in your own suffering. If you would be honest with yourself, you have played a part in the areas you have suffered or are suffering in. Sometimes, your own thoughts, feelings, and actions can rob you of your happiness, healing, and peace. I can remember in some of the most painful seasons I was going through, I would try to express how I was feeling, thinking I was going to get some compassion and see change, and that wasn't the case. I was told that you could be healed today; that was like adding salt to an open wound. I was still internally wounded, trying to recover. And one day, God spoke to me and said daughter, you get to decide how long you will stay in that place. That was my turning point. I decided to take control, no longer allowing negative responses to trigger me. I found out that it definitely takes grit to change.

I began to walk towards my healing. It's impossible to stay the victim and walk in victory. That's when I realized every closed wound isn't a healed wound. A closed wound will often leave bruises from the impact of a fall or hard hit. It's a wound that I discovered will never break the skin but will break the heart, and I had to confront the pain from the power of conflict. Conflict in a relationship can cause long-lasting effects if allowed. The hard hits from words spoken out of anger can pierce the heart, causing internal bleeding, which can leave you physically and emotionally bound. The things that trigger the negative emotions will show you your level of growth and the need for spiritual transformation. And only through His Word will you be able to measure the depth of your healing by your own actions.

Learning to turn the other cheek, not spitting back at someone who spits at you, speaking well of someone who speaks ill of you, and responding by applying His word to circumstances shows a renewed mindset. When you renew your mind, it's an inward process that leads to sanctification and transformation, which shows conversion. What is conversion? Conversion is daily repentance; it's change, turning away from your own belief systems, adopting a new life and a new way of living by not copying the behavior and customs of this world, but letting God transform you into a new person by changing the way you think. *"Then you will learn to know God's will for you, which is good and pleasing and perfect"* (Romans 12:2, NLT).

Renewing the mind is a daily task. Transitioning isn't easy. You must be willing to be uncomfortable to be comfortable. You must push past old behavior and beliefs. You must not be afraid to reset to set new boundaries, and you must give yourself permission to hit the reset button. It is okay not to be okay, and it's definitely okay to let go and be free, my friends. Your reset is more about you becoming a new creation in Christ and a better you. When you allow the Word of God to transform you, you will understand that tests and trials are all prerequisites to walking in your purpose. You will look at the pain and who caused it differently.

I learned my process really had nothing to do with my "baby daddy," it was my process, and I realized my healing was my responsibility. I had to hit my reset button. I promise this will happen when you are sick and tired of being in the same place and condition. I was waiting for him to do something for me that only I could do. And the truth of the matter is all I needed to do was "get up, pick up my mat (your mat represents the issues of your heart and soul), and walk," applying my faith. In John 5:8, the man at the Pool of Bethesda, also known as the "house of mercy", was lame for thirty-eight long years waiting for someone to help him get healed. He began to complain and make excuses that someone would come and get ahead of him every time he wanted to get in the pool. The danger of waiting on someone or putting our healing in someone else's hands is it may never happen; they may never ask you for forgiveness, and they may never help you heal. This does not negate nor excuse all those who have purposely caused some type of pain or disappointment in your or my life. But what it shows is that you and I can enter a mature place where we can forgive them, forgive ourselves, and ask to be forgiven. I was no longer angry, bitter, or resentful towards him or my process. I finally realized he couldn't give me what he didn't have, and I'm not talking about anything material. Only God can teach you how to be a godly husband or godly wife, and you have to be willing to admit you don't know how, letting all pride and ego go.

I now bear more fruit because I decided to grow and be mature amid adversity. I had to learn how to take my thoughts captive by reading and meditating on scripture and spending time in His presence, and it caused me to see and hear out of the eyes and ears of the spirit. This couldn't have been done without God's help. Time does heal all wounds when you take action. How do you know you're healed and whole? You know you are healed when you can look back at what wounded you, and you are now grateful and thankful for it all, and you do not take the healing power of God for granted. When you are whole, you and others can witness that you have found your new identity from your brokenness and that you have been conformed to the image of God by His love and participation and "your actions." Being whole will allow you to walk in your freedom. I rejoice in my freedom and in the fact that we are able to co-parent well. He loves our daughter, and she is indeed a daddy's girl. We are able to laugh and love each other as brother and sister in Christ and respect each other as friends. A prayer answered! I survived to make an impact. I surely thought many times that the results would have been me in prison with a prison ministry or sitting in a padded room in a mental institution. Oh, but Jesus! There is so much power in those words alone. Every obstacle becomes powerless when Jesus enters!

Often our reset is for us but not about us. God is not just concerned about our physical healing but about the spiritual and the condition of our hearts. Can God trust you to have a heart of repentance and a heart that forgives? Can God have permission to stretch you and your faith? Can God trust you long enough to stay in the fire to learn who and what you are called to? Our conversion and calling are found in the fire of life! The called ones are the ones that will follow God through the fire and the ones who will obey in the difficult seasons of life.

"For many are called but a few are chosen" (Matthew 22:14, KJV). How do we know if we are chosen? It is the one that has an ear to hear the call. It is the one who hears and obeys even when you know it will be painful to your flesh. When you answer and obey the call, that is when you will have a head-on collision with your purpose. Your purpose is what you have been created for. The calling is the long road you take to get to the purpose. Your purpose is your final destination in your own personal journey. You cannot get there without experience. The

experiences and lessons from the detours and the roadblocks will prepare you for the impacts you will make because you answered the call. God will always complete the scene bringing your story to a full circle and allowing you to hit the reset button, giving you a fresh new start. Forget about what has happened, do not keep going over old history. *"Be alert, be present. I am about to do something brand new. It's bursting out! Don't you see it?"* (Isaiah 43:19, MSG).

After I've suffered for a little while, I can look at every scar and give God praise that I made it out. If you are going through any situations that are beyond your control, you will make it out. God will take all the broken pieces in your life and put them back together again. And you will say as I said, *"It was good for me that I had been afflicted that I may learn of your statutes"* (Psalm 119:71, KJV). I found out that God will never remove you from the problem until He builds you in the problem. God is in the reset business. Focus on what is important (Jesus). Stay in position to be launched into your next. You are not defined by what happened to you. "Get up, take up your mat, and walk" boldly and unapologetically in your healing.

YOU ARE NOT A FAILURE

∼

There will be times you will look at your situation and begin to think that you are a failure. You are not a failure. You may have failed at something, but it doesn't make you a failure. There were times that I felt like I was a failure until I changed the way I was thinking (mindset). Not seeing myself as a failure allowed me to turn a setback into a major comeback (reset). You may ask if I wanted my marriage to work. Absolutely, I wanted my marriage to work; I wanted until death do us part, but I could no longer allow time vested to outweigh me being loved the way I desired to be loved, simply because I know who I am, and I know my worth. Staying in unhealthy and toxic relationships with unchecked narcissistic behavior will be a life with no peace and no agreement. When you lose agreement, you lose power. Lost power is lost respect and victory. And I don't believe it is God's desire for us to remain in those types of relationships unless counseling or therapy is done and there is change, and if not, He gives us free will to make choices and the peace to go with it. However, it is a known fact that God will sometimes allow the closest to us to scar us the most. I had to accept what was; I learned that failure has lessons attached to it. Every time you fail, you learn. And one of the first lessons I learned was that I was only in control of my growth. As bad as I wanted him to grow, it was not my job to force that or to speak against his growth but to take ownership of my own.

My second lesson was that the fear of failing will keep you in situations that no longer benefit you because you want something to live that God has allowed to die. I may have failed at some things in my marriage, but my personal belief will always be I was a darn good wife, and in knowing that, I was able to walk away knowing I did my best. So do not let the fear of failure, defeat, or shame paralyze you, but yet build your confidence and be resilient in the face of adversity. We will not be able to stop or change the challenges that God allows to come in our life, but we can change how we look at them, and how we look at them will change our outcome. Keep persevering. There is something greater on the other side. With every ending, there is a new beginning awaiting you.

"For God hath not given you a spirit of fear, but of power, and of love, and of a sound mind" (2 Timothy 1:7, KJV). You are anointed for the hard things. Just believe, "I can do all things (which He has called me to do) through Him who strengthens and empowers me (to fulfill His purpose-I am self-sufficient in Christ's sufficiency); I am ready for anything and equal to anything through Him who infuses me with inner strength and confident peace" (Philippians 4:13, AMP).

CHAPTER 6

Elevation Is Undeniable

~

"I see what you have done. Now see what I've done. I opened a door before you that no man can slam shut. You do not have much strength; I know that; You used what you had to keep my Word. You did not deny me when times were rough."

(Revelations 3:8, MSG)

No demon in hell can stop the plan of God! Your elevation is undeniable when you remain faithful to God in the fire. You cannot be denied. Tough times will not last, but tough people will. Your miracle is found in the fire. I remember begging God to remove me from my process because the fire was so intense, and I felt like I couldn't take it anymore. I really thought He would save me from the fire, but He saved me in the fire. When you persevere in persecution and don't deny Him in tough times or bow to other gods, God will provide unimaginable "open doors" (blessings). He will use the challenges and obstacles that the enemy thought would destroy you as stepping stones. God has always been acquainted with the who, what, how, and the why of His people.

In the scripture mentioned above, He is speaking to the Church of Philadelphia, one of the seven churches, which means (brotherly love). This church was a group of believers who had little power but great influence and who were found faithful in suffering and being persecuted by the Jews, also known as the "synagogue of Satan" (slanders). The slanders were being used to torment them, but they didn't know it was actually elevating them. The enemy is so dumb; he doesn't realize when he messes with us that it actually provokes us to our destiny, which is why you can't let him see you sweat or stay down too long. The enemy planned to apply so much pressure that it would cause them to drop out of the race, which is still Satan's plan for you and me today. He wants us to be intimidated by his tactics and drop out of the race before we see elevation. He doesn't know when he turns up the heat, God does too. There were plenty of times that I thought the enemy would win while going through my process.

God will never allow our enemies to triumph over us. When you choose to endure patiently, He will make all liars come and fall at your feet, making your enemies your footstool. When going through the most challenging seasons of your life, the enemy will come with all kinds of lies, trying to make you second guess who you are and even question if God loves you. I found out repeatedly that He was madly in love with me and reassured me there was a purpose behind my pain and promotion behind the pressure. I found out that I wasn't crazy for what I believed because what I believed was from His Word, and His Word is true. The Church of Philadelphia was blessed because they kept His word in hard times. They were a loyal, committed group of believers who weren't alarmed by the enemy. We must remember he has no new tricks. He's a deceiver with no truth found in him. He heightens and intensifies the same tricks; his objectives will always be to discourage you, distract you, keep you bound in fear, make you worry about things out of your control, and make you doubt what God said. Don't you fall prey to his lies. God rules! Elevation comes from God. *"For not from the east, or from the west, nor from the wilderness [is} elevation. It is God alone who judges; He decides who will rise and who will fall* (Psalm 75: 6-7, NLT). All elevation is God orchestrated and is designed to reposition you. Every valley moment has a purpose in your elevation. In the valley, you will discover that your come-up is based on God alone, that nothing will be done in your own strength.

The danger in elevation is when you try to do it yourself by rushing the process. Learn to "wait" on God's timing. Not waiting will result in unnecessary disappointments and setbacks. *"Those that wait upon the Lord shall renew their strength. They shall mount up with wings of eagles they shall run and not be weary, and they shall walk and not faint"* (Isaiah 40:29-31, KJV).

The Hebrew word for wait is "qavah," which means waiting, looking for, hoping, expecting to collect, and bonding together. There is something that should be happening in the waiting process. That is, becoming one with the Father through Intimacy= Into Me You See! You must wait on God, stay in His presence, and become one with Him so that your character will reflect His and you are prepared to handle the elevation. Once again, don't get out of the fire too soon. After the fire, the king promoted the three Hebrew boys, they came out of the fire not looking like smoke, smelling like smoke, and their hair was not singed, and they were elevated. That is my testimony! There will be no evidence that you were in the fiery furnace. All because Jesus the chain breaker was in the fire with you. I wouldn't wish my fire experience on an enemy. But the elevation I received from it will allow me to extend the same grace I received and pray for my enemies. Doing this empowers heaven to move on our behalf. That's why you must understand forgiveness is for you. Before Job was promoted and restored, there were several things he needed to get right, and one of them was to pray for his accusers, haters, naysayers, backbiters, or whatever you want to call those so-called friends. When he prayed, the Lord turned the captivity of Job, and he received twice as much, open door blessings. That's why you must be careful who you call friends and stay aware of those who call themselves supporters but are trying to get close to you, only wanting what you have. You know, the ones who want to walk in someone else's shoes because you have made it look easy and you don't look like what you've been through, so they want to be you. Oh well! Sorry to say, you will fail and fall every time. It's only one of you, no carbon copies. Your anointing is yours for a reason. You paid a hell of a price for it. You don't know the cost of the oil in their alabaster box. You weren't there to see the many nights they cried. But you will see the elevation. The doors He opens, no man can shut.

CHAPTER 7

The Divine Assignment

~

"I will instruct you and teach in the way you should go; I will counsel you with my loving eye on you."

(Psalm 32:8, NIV)

God has a specific plan and purpose for each of our lives. To fulfill your divine assignment, you must know and understand God's Word. It is through His Word that He will guide and instruct us to know His will. He will never change His Word or say anything against what He has already spoken concerning you or the assignment. His Word is true, and there is no contradiction in it. The problem God created you to solve here on earth is called "your assignment." Assign means to be set apart for a special purpose, mission, or task. What you and I have been assigned to will allow us to solve problems and add value. This will not come about without persecutions, trials, and tribulations. Your scars emotionally, physically, and mentally will be a constant reminder of the weight you carry. The weight of His glory that I carry now did not come easy, and neither will yours. It cost me, and it is still costing me, to be honest. But it has allowed me to solve problems and add value to others out of my obedience to Him and the Cross.

Let's look at some of the problem solvers in the Word. Jesus solved problems, not absent of the Cross. Joseph solved problems, not absent of the pit. Daniel solved problems, not absent from the lion's den. The three Hebrew boys solved problems, not absent from the fiery furnace. Mary solved the biggest problem, not absent of shame, giving birth to our Savior, all while being espoused to Joseph. She was given this assignment, and she was the only one that was chosen to solve that problem. Imagine the gossip that was going on about her, engaged but pregnant by another man. Your assignment can make you look crazy and very well be unexplainable when God is in it. It will make no sense to you, but your divine assignment is set up for you and only you. You must fulfill your assignment on earth, for when night comes, no man can work.

God allowing me to be broken inside of my marriage allowed me to grow in Christ and has afforded me the opportunity to speak into the lives of those going through toxic relationships, dysfunctional marriages, divorces, separation, hurting and abused women. To pastors' wives who are secretly suffering in silence, I went through for you, and I am here for all of my sisters in this position (there is hope). I can speak to those who have experienced a miscarriage, those that have been fondled as a child or teenager, those that have gone through financial hardship, bankruptcy, or foreclosure, and those that are caregivers to their loved ones, how to live a single and saved life, entrepreneurship, and how not to quit. I survived my season of testing. There are some things I have not been assigned to because I have not paid that price. If you have not paid the price and have not gone through the process, save your opinions! Opinions have never set anyone free; only the anointing can set you free, with the yoke destroying power of God, so if you haven't been endowed with power or anointed to speak on it, save your opinions.

If you are single and have never been married, do not try to tell a married person how to be a wife. Instead, walk into your assignment regardless of how small it may seem to you. No assignment is too small or insignificant when you look at your God-given assignment through the lens of an omnipotent God. So be a good steward and master the level that you are on.

Someone's blood is attached to your hands. You walking in your assignment will cause someone else to live. Be faithful to your assignment regardless of whether it is to one person or a multitude. When I finally figured out my purpose and who I was assigned to, I was literally clueless at the fact that my purpose was connected to what I was passionate about. I was given a talent to enhance individuals' outer beauty but going through my process groomed me to help aid them in their inner beauty as well. God takes what we are passionate about and merges it with purpose to make it sustainable. Passion is for you; it's what drives you. Your purpose is for others, while both are essential for growth. Walking in your purpose will change your life, and the people around you will begin to change. God allowed me to serve in ministry in every salon I worked in and even in my own. I was prophesying, laying hands, leading people to Christ, and sadly partaking in some of their homegoings. I was doing marketplace ministry before I was fully aware that's what I was doing. You must be willing to lead wherever you are placed. Marketplace ministry is a part of God's strategic plan. It is the ministry that happens outside of the four walls of the church. Some of my clients were not churchgoers, and others did not attend regularly. Their lives were touched all because of Him and me yielding to my painful process. He gets all the glory!

The running joke by one of my colleagues at Boz & Co. says I was in the club one minute and saved the next; that is too funny, it seemed that way, but the process was long (long-suffering). The other amazing part was a lot of people He had me ministering to were the ones I clubbed with. That says a lot. When God gets you where He wants you, you will go back to minister to and pray for the same ones you partied with. Until then, be faithful in your field, tending to the one, two, or three sheep before you are given the stage? Every stage you are called to, you must be prepared for. The first stage he gave me was for my family. They were the first ones I began to share my journey with, ensuring they understood that hell and heaven are real and receiving salvation is the only assurance to make heaven your home. Ministry first starts in the home. I can only pray that they have been inspired and impacted by my walk in Christ. I am not perfect, but I am God's child, and I have been consistent with my walk. There was no greater joy than being an inspiration to my mom, dad, grandparents, and other family members. Some received Christ as their personal savior, and others were challenged to grow deeper in their walk all because of my yes to the Cross and my assignment.

I remember so clearly my mom seeing me after a women's fellowship I was attending on Mondays with my cousin, Patsy, who was older than I, and some older season saints. (I love hanging around older people, so much wisdom.) I remember going by her house after being in the presence of the Lord and experiencing Him as I had never experienced Him before. I went one way, and my chair went another way that night; it was one of the nights marked in my salvation history that left me in complete awe, never having to question the power of

God. The fire of God was all over me, and when I got to my mom's house, she knew something was different. I recall hearing her saying, "Daughter, I want what you got." She had seen the residue of His glory upon me, and the crazy part is at that time, my mom's boyfriend was living with her. In her sin, she saw His glory and was willing to walk away from that relationship, and God did a quick work in her, and she received Christ and received the baptism of the Holy Spirit with the evidence of speaking in tongues. What a testimony! (This story is a tearjerker). The same one that witnessed my death, burial, and resurrection, is now my prayer warrior and intercessor, all because I answered the call. I can go on and on to bring glory to God. You will never find true success in life until you discover and embrace your purpose.

You will discover your purpose as you continue to walk through the painful uncertainties of life. There is purpose in your pain, confusion, and chaos. You can only make an impact through adversity. God allows adversities to build resilience and increase our faith. There was a time when I thought I had done something so bad in my life that caused the suffering that I was experiencing, and that was not the case. Yes, you can suffer for being disobedient, but not all our discipline from God is because we did something bad. God uses adversity as a training ground for spiritual growth. He allowed that divine darkness and delay in my life for me to develop a deeper fellowship with Him so that when He called me for my assignment, I would know His voice. A stranger to His voice will never hear the call, but one in deep communion with Him will hear it, even if you don't want to answer it. Could the reason you don't know your assignment or your purpose be because you haven't allowed your suffering to bring you into deeper communion with Him? You are so focused on the attacks from the enemy that you don't see that God has allowed the attacks for you to reestablish total dependency on Him. When life hits you, you immediately become isolated, afraid to engage in spiritual warfare. You must understand that spiritual warfare has so many benefits; it was never intended wholeheartedly to be used just against our adversary but to clear the way for deeper revelation and communion with God (worship). When you lose sight of what the enemy is doing and focus on God, you will once again find the grace that will empower you to do what you could've never done on your own. God restores when you develop a daily life of communing with Him and not just on Sunday mornings.

I stand amazed; I marvel at His goodness. He chose a little ole girl named Shonda aka Shon, to some, (Lol! Don't call me that unless you've been around me for years) with her past childhood insecurities, hurt, failures, disappointments, shame, and inadequacies to be in this place of freedom, saying like Job, I don't just know Him, but I've seen Him with my own eyes. I can boldly say that when I wake up, Satan says to his imps, *"Let's run, she's up* because I understand my spiritual authority now, and it's because of the hardship I endured. NOBODY BUT JESUS! Please lift your hands right here and receive my prayer for you.

Father, I thank You for my brother or sister as they lift their hands towards Heaven as a sign of surrender. I pray that You will grace them in this defining moment in their life. I ask that You give them Holy Ghost boldness to live in their truth and give them the strength to endure hardship as a good soldier. I ask that they exit their process, not looking like what they have gone through. I pray that they will be obedient to the Cross and their assignment. I come against the adversary that seeks to steal, kill, and destroy. I decree and declare they will not die; instead, they live to tell what the Lord has done and that through their transparency, someone will decide to live in Jesus' name! Amen.

I promise you; that this was not an accident. I'm alive because there is so much more in store for me. Grace got me through it! *"My grace is sufficient for you; my strength is made perfect in weakness"* (2 Corinthians 12:9, NKJV). Your scars were intentional! You were scarred for ("4") purpose on purpose. The number four (4) is very significant in the Bible. It signifies the beginning of a new era in life and God's perfect creative ability and complete work (wholeness). You are His perfect creation. On the fourth day, God said, "Let there be light- bearers" (sun, moon, stars) to separate the day from the night, let them mark the seasons, days, and the years. The sun, moon, and stars were created to give light to the world and divide the days. Sunshines, you are the light-bearers (light of the world), a city set on a hill that cannot be hidden. Let your light shine before others so that they may see your good works and give glory to your Father, who is in heaven. He created you to be the salt of the earth. You are the one that gives divine flavor. He created you to be His witness (mouthpiece) to testify of His goodness and to preach in season and out of season (to prove that He exists). May you walk boldly in your light (your testimony of the truth of Christ) and your salt (the character of Christ), your wholeness, and your God-given assignment. When you see the number four, may you constantly be reminded of how perfect and powerful (omnipotent) God is and that you are His creative being. When connected to Him, you are capable of doing anything, greater works.

"Truly, truly, I say to you, whoever believes in me will also do the works that I do; greater works than these will he do because I am going to the Father." (John 14:12, ESV)

PEARLS OF WISDOM

- ❖ Surrender to Christ.

- ❖ Believe in Him.

- ❖ Go through God's process of transformation and maturation.

- ❖ Seek the Holy Spirit through fasting and praying to know and understand your assignment.

- ❖ Be empowered by the Holy Spirit to do the assignment.

- ❖ Your obedience to your assignment will create a path for others.

CHAPTER 8

The Unstoppable You

~

"Don't interfere with good people's lives; don't try to get the best of them. No matter how many times you trip them up, loyal people don't stay down long. Soon they're up on their feet, while the wicked end up flat on their faces."

(Proverbs 24:15-16, MSG)

Dear hearts, you are unstoppable; you are a force to be reckoned with; you are valuable; stop underestimating your worth and devaluing your presence. Your presence is powerful; it causes demons to tremble, and there is not one person, demon, weapon, or tongue that can stop you. Remember, what you see as valuable; others will value. You are an asset. You add value to life. You are needed. You are His "treasured possession," the apple of His eye, fashioned in His image (fearfully and wonderfully made). It is impossible to stop someone who God has put His stamp of approval on. You cannot accept defeat, nor will you be defeated because it's not in your spiritual DNA. Just believe you have what it takes to keep going. As a born-again believer, you have the spiritual stamina to endure hardship. The Bible tells us to *"endure hardships as a good soldier"* (2 Timothy 2:3, KJV). You have been given the power to endure unpleasant situations. Being unstoppable has nothing to do with you or your capabilities. So never throw "unstoppable" around unless you understand the power that works in you! Now unto Him who is able to (carry out His purpose) do superabundantly more than all that we dare ask or think (infinitely beyond our greatest prayers, hopes, or dreams) according to "His power" that is at work within us. To Him be the glory in the church and in Christ Jesus throughout all generations forever and ever. Amen. (Ephesians 3:20-21, AMP)

Let me elaborate more on this. The Holy Spirit leads us, strengthens us, and comforts us. Our power comes from the Holy Spirit. So, without the Holy Spirit, we are like Superman without his cape, Wonder Woman without her intellect or bracelets. Without the Holy Spirit, we are powerless. So then, the power that is given to us, we must choose to use it. He gives us the ability to be unstoppable because His Spirit dwells in us. Genesis 1:26 says it best, *"Let us make man in our image,"* which tells us that the Holy Spirit is already in us. So, our job is to receive Jesus Christ as our personal Savior, be filled with the Holy Spirit, and activate the power (Holy Spirit) in us. He is a gentleman, so He'll never force Himself on you, so you will have to employ Him, put Him to work by asking in prayer. The same spirit that hovered over the face of the earth and backed up God's Word to create light in a dark world is the same power in us. When walking habitually in the Holy Spirit and not our flesh, He will help keep us from carrying out the desires of our sinful nature (Galatians 5:16, AMP). Our process is designed to give us power over our sin, get rid of ways that don't please Him, and keep us "mindful" that we need Him to be "unstoppable." The King empowers us to live a life without limitations.

Those who know me know that I am a pearly girl. I love pearls, and I grew to appreciate them more through my process. I discovered some interesting things about the oyster: it travels alone and travels throughout the sea, minding its business. Its mission is to make sure the water is healthy. The oyster is a natural filter that improves water, overloaded with nutrients as it goes about its day. When it is greeted by an intruder, a parasite, or a grain of sand gets between its shells, it begins to cover the irritating object with nacre (mother of pearl) layers upon layers to protect itself from the unwanted intruder until the pearl is made. That is so powerful because I also believe a man or woman who prays over the things that irritate them, covering them in layers of prayer, will yield results. Taking time to pray and praying in the spirit (tongues) will activate the power in you that makes you unstoppable.

I also want to convey that the oyster never stops going about its business, fulfilling its mission, although irritated. It keeps moving about, applying pressure. The only way to stop a wound from bleeding is to apply pressure. Applying pressure will produce the unimaginable in your life. The most fashionable and elaborate piece of jewelry that women love to wear is developed from the pressure applied by the oyster. You must be like an oyster; keep applying the pressure until you see what God said. I once heard that an oyster that has never been injured would never produce pearls because the pearl indicates a healed wound. Don't let that temporary irritation cause you to stay down. Get your bounce back, soldier.

The enemy hates to see you bounce back. I admit my bounce back was deliberate; I had too many watching, wanting to see me stay down, and too many that needed me to get up. I felt like the weeble wobble toy we played with as a child. "Weebles wobble, but they don't fall down." I often wondered why it never fell down, and I found out it is weighted on the bottom. They were designed to withstand the hits, kicks, pushes, and forceful hold-downs and always bounced back. The weebles represent the resilience one must have in life. No matter how many times you may experience falling or being knocked down, be like that weeble wobble and bounce back.

God's weight is in you; you are weighted. And oh, by the way (just a little FYI), your purpose will not let you quit or stay down; you will never be at peace until it's fulfilled. All the wounds from your life you thought would kill you only carved a pathway for you to live. You have the spiritual DNA of an overcomer on the inside of you. *"In this world, you will have trouble. But take heart! I have overcome the world"* (John 16:33, NIV). I reiterate to you again; you will not be stopped. Dream, believe, and hope again, pursue that career, write that book, and start that business. You owe this win to yourself! And the way you're going to win is by having the confidence to believe in God's plan and your abilities, qualities, and judgment to follow the plan through.

I would like to end with this. The world is your oyster. You have been created to thrive in difficult situations. You have been scarred for purpose on purpose. At the end of Job's story (Chapter 42:1-2, GW), Job confesses that he was wrong, *"Then Job answered the Lord, 'I know that you can do everything and that your plans are UNSTOPPABLE.'"* God's plans for your life are unstoppable.

You are getting ready to give birth to something bigger and greater than you!

Conclusion

You may be suffering, and you may have taken some hard blows. But be not dismayed. Sometimes you have to lose to win again. God has strategically set your scene. You were chosen to go through whatever you may be experiencing or have experienced, including all the trauma and the drama. It was predestined and a part of you before you were placed in your mother's womb. Every test and trial you will encounter, He will use to build character and use for His glory. Stay in the race, jump your hurdles (the obstacles set before you), and don't abort the process. This process is for you and you only. The moment you start asking Him to change your situation and others around you, you have invited God in to start changing you.

What you are going through isn't about them but you. Let go of the past hurt, disappointments, bitterness, and anger; forgive them and yourself and let God remodel (make you over), and hit that reset button (change your mindset). Stay yielded, continue to endure hardship as a good soldier, and remain committed to the process.

The process will help you discover your purpose, what you were created for, and who you have been called to. Your place of exile (cave) was temporary; it prepared you for your promise. The promise is a place of rest. Abide in peace, continue to grow in holiness, and elevation will be undeniable to you; your elevation is for the divine assignment that is attached to the pain you endured. Although pain is never pleasurable, it will allow you to walk in power and wisdom.

God has given you what you need to live a life without limits. You are His Masterpiece, His work of art, and you are UNSTOPPABLE!

I pray that something was said in my transparency to help you understand that your wounds, scabs, and scars have a purpose. Every wound has wisdom; every scab will allow you to experience His grace, and every scar has power and purpose attached to it. Dear hearts, get ready for God to bestow upon you a crown of beauty instead of ashes, the oil of joy instead of mourning, and a garment of praise instead of a spirit of heaviness. To Him be the glory forever and ever. Amen!

Salvation Prayer

If you are reading this book and you have not accepted Jesus Christ as your personal Savior, or you're in a backslidden place, please repeat this prayer and don't miss out on the benefits of serving El Elyon (The Most High God).

Heavenly Father, I repent of my sins. I thank You for allowing Your Son to die in my stead. I confess with my mouth that Jesus is Lord, and I believe in my heart that God has raised Him from the dead, and I shall be saved. For with the heart, man believes unto righteousness, and with the mouth, confession is made unto salvation in Jesus' name! I want to welcome you into the family, and the entire heaven is rejoicing over your decision. Thank You, Lord, for my new brother and sister!

GRACEFULLY BROKEN, and BEAUTIFULLY SCARRED

About the Author

Shonda Boyd Brown has been called to the kingdom for such a time as this. An only child, mother of one beautiful daughter, and a mentor to many, she has a heart for God's people. As a licensed and ordained Evangelist and Elder, she has been in ministry for 20 years. She gives all the glory to God as the Holy Spirit has definitely been her best teacher. Shonda Boyd Brown has served in numerous capacities in ministry. She is called to the masses, focusing on women's ministry. She is a licensed cosmetologist and educator in North Carolina and a licensed master stylist in Georgia with 30 years as an entrepreneur in the beauty industry. She traveled across the states as a platform artist and is featured in magazines and many hair influencers' social media pages. She is the founder and Chief Executive Officer (CEO) of Divine Creations, Divine Institute 4 Hair, Zee's Tees by Divine Fashion Gallery, and Women Impact Nations women's ministry (W...I...N). She firmly believes that knowing who you are and whose you are is a prerequisite to boldly walking in the "GODFIDENCE" needed to pursue your divine purpose. Her mission is to spread the love of JESUS CHRIST through her transparency and win souls for the KINGDOM of GOD.

www.ingramcontent.com/pod-product-compliance
Lightning Source LLC
Chambersburg PA
CBHW050300120526
44590CB00016B/2425